EVERYWHERE I LOOK is a collection of essays, diary entries and true stories spanning more than fifteen years of the work of one of Australia's greatest writers. Helen Garner takes us from backstage at the ballet to the trial of a woman for infanticide, from the significance of moving house to the pleasure of re-reading *Pride and Prejudice*. The collection includes her famous and controversial essay on the insults of age, her deeply moving tribute to her mother, and the story of her joy in discovering the ukulele. *Everywhere I Look* is a multifaceted, profound portrait of life. It glows with insight and wisdom.

PRAISE FOR HELEN GARNER

'Garner is one of those wonderful writers whose voice one hears and whose eyes one sees through. Her style, conversational but never slack, is natural, supple and exact, her way of seeing is acute and sympathetic, you receive an instant impression of being in the company of a congenial friend and it is impossible not to follow her as she brings to life the events and feelings she is exploring.'
Diana Athill

'A voice of great honesty and energy.'
Anne Enright

'Scrupulously objective and profoundly personal.'
Kate Atkinson

'Garner's spare, clean style flowers into magnificent poetry.'
Australian Book Review

'She has a Jane Austen–like ability to whizz an arrow straight into the truest depths of human nature, including her own.'
Life Sentence

'Compassionate and dispassionate in equal measure…She writes with a profound understanding of human vulnerability, and of the subtle workings of love, memory and remorse.'
Economist

'Helen Garner's greatest skill is to encourage the reader not to make judgment but to listen.'
Australian

'She watches, imagines, second-guesses, empathises, agonises. Her voice—intimate yet sharp, wry yet urgent—inspires trust.'
Atlantic

'Garner's writing [is] so assured and compassionate that any reader will be enthralled and swept along.'
Australian Bookseller & Publisher

'The words almost dance off the page.'
Launceston Examiner

'Garner is a beautiful writer who winkles out difficult emotions from difficult hiding places.'
Sunday Telegraph

'Her use of language is sublime.'
Scotsman

'Garner writes with a fearsome, uplifting grace.'
Metro UK

'A combination of wit and lyricism that is immensely alluring.'
Observer

'Honest, unsparing and brave.'
New York Times

'There's no denying the force of her storytelling.'
Telegraph

ALSO BY HELEN GARNER

FICTION

Monkey Grip

Honour and Other People's Children

The Children's Bach

Postcards from Surfers

Cosmo Cosmolino

The Spare Room

NON-FICTION

The First Stone

True Stories

The Feel of Steel

Joe Cinque's Consolation

This House of Grief

SCREENPLAYS

The Last Days of Chez Nous

Two Friends

Helen Garner was born in Geelong in 1942. Her books include novels, stories, screenplays and works of non-fiction.

HELEN GARNER
EVERYWHERE I LOOK

TEXT PUBLISHING MELBOURNE AUSTRALIA

The Text Publishing Company
Swann House
22 William Street
Melbourne Victoria 3000
Australia
textpublishing.com.au

First published in Australia by The Text Publishing Company, 2016.

Many of the stories in this collection have been previously published. See page 229 for details.

Lines on p. 102 from *An Experiment in Love*, Viking, 1995, © Hilary Mantel 1995, reproduced with permission.

Book & cover design by W. H. Chong
Cover photograph by Darren James
Typeset by J&M Typesetters
Printed and bound in Australia by Griffin Press, an Accredited ISO AS/NZS 14001:2004 Environmental Management System printer

National Library of Australia Cataloguing-in-Publication

Creator: Garner, Helen, 1942– author.

Title: Everywhere I look / by Helen Garner.

ISBN: 9781925355369 (paperback)

ISBN: 9781922253644 (ebook)

Subjects: Garner, Helen, 1942–

Garner, Helen, 1942—Criticism and interpretation.

Garner, Helen, 1942—Diaries.

Authorship.

Life.

Dewey Number: A823.3

This book is printed on paper certified against the Forest Stewardship Council® Standards. Griffin Press holds FSC chain-of-custody certification SGS-COC-005088. FSC promotes environmentally responsible, socially beneficial and economically viable management of the world's forests.

EVERYWHERE I LOOK

CONTENTS

PART ONE: WHITE PAINT AND CALICO

Whisper and Hum   3
Some Furniture   7
White Paint and Calico   11
Suburbia   20

PART TWO: NOTES FROM A BRIEF FRIENDSHIP

Dear Mrs Dunkley   29
Eight Views of Tim Winton   34
Notes from a Brief Friendship   40
From Frogmore, Victoria   47
My Dear Lift-Rat   58

PART THREE: DREAMS OF HER REAL SELF

While Not Writing a Book: Diary 1   65
Red Dog: A Mutiny   78
Funk Paradise: Diary 2   82
Dreams of Her Real Self   90
Before Whatever Else Happens: Diary 3   106

PART FOUR: ON DARKNESS

Punishing Karen   121
The Singular Rosie   126
The City at Night   133
The Man in the Dock   137
On Darkness   141

PART FIVE: THE JOURNEY OF THE STAMP ANIMALS

The Journey of the Stamp Animals   155
Worse Things than Writers Can Invent   158
How to Marry Your Daughters   161
X-ray of a Pianist at Work   167
Gall and Barefaced Daring   170
The Rules of Engagement   176
The Rapture of Firsthand Encounters   181
Hit Me   185

PART SIX: IN THE WINGS

My First Baby   197
Big Brass Bed   201
Dawn Service   204
A Party   207
The Insults of Age   211
In the Wings   218

PART ONE
White Paint and Calico

Whisper and Hum

WHEN I was in my forties I went on holiday to Vanuatu with a kind and very musical man to whom I would not much longer be married, though I didn't know it yet.

He was at ease in the Pacific climate, but I hated the tropics with a passion: all that sweating and melting and shapelessness and blurring. And what I hated most was the sight of a certain parasitic creeper that flourished aggressively, bowing the treetops down and binding them to each other in a dense, undifferentiated mat of choking foliage. I longed to be transported at once to Scotland where the air was sharp and the nights brisk, and where plants were encouraged to grow separately and upright, with individual dignity.

At nightfall the whole population of the island would walk into town, and so would my restless husband and his discontented wife. In velvety air and under a starry sky, a stream of people padded along a sandy track, quietly chattering and laughing.

One evening a Melanesian man in torn and baggy clothes was walking on his own in front of us. He seemed to be cradling something small against his chest. Occasionally he lowered his face over it. We heard faint rhythmic music, and when we passed him we saw that he was playing a tiny stringed instrument, strumming it very softly as he swung along by himself in the cheerful crowd. He wasn't performing, or wanting anyone else to hear what he was doing. He was playing just to keep himself company.

I wanted one of those instruments. I wanted to hold it in my arms.

I crushed this longing with my usual puritanical savagery. You're too old. You couldn't even learn the piano. You have no musical talent. You will make a fool of yourself and everyone will laugh at you. Pull yourself together, woman, and slog on.

But when we got home to Melbourne I took down the *Oxford Companion to Music* and looked up the ukulele. 'It has four strings and a very long fingerboard…It was patented in Honolulu in 1917, from which date it gradually became popular in the United States amongst *people whose desire to perform was stronger than their willingness to acquire any difficult technique or their desire to make intimate acquaintance with any very elaborate music.*'

So. It was a cop-out for the lazy and talentless. I went straight downtown and bought the first one I saw that didn't look trashy. It was made in Czechoslovakia and it cost $45. I also bought Mel Bay's *You Can Teach Yourself Uke*. I put them in a cupboard under a pile of blankets and said nothing about them to anyone.

Whenever I was home alone I would rush upstairs and take the uke out of its cardboard box. It was so intimate, so un-awe-inspiring, with its curvaceous waist and pretty metal frets and creamy tuning pegs. A faint perfume drifted out of its woody little body. And, unlike the hulking piano which years earlier had brought me to my knees, it was small. No one could possibly be afraid of this instrument. I fell in love with it. I spent secret afternoons sitting on the bed strumming my way through the beginner's book. I learnt 'Row, Row, Row Your Boat' and 'Camptown Races'. It was easy. It was natural. Four strings, four fingers, not like a guitar, where you're ganged up on every time you try to make a chord.

I found I could learn a three-chord song in about thirty seconds. It dawned on me that there are several million three-chord songs in the world, many of which I had effortlessly, long ago, stored in the mud at the very bottom of my memory. Up they came from the depths, dripping and sparkling—so fresh, shining with common human feeling. And I saw that the ukulele, despite the snotty entry in the Oxford Companion, has in fact a simple and benevolent purpose: to create a gentle bed of sound for the human voice; to enrich the single line of melody that a human voice is capable of.

Somewhere in the background of all this, my marriage crashed and my daughter grew up and left home. Next time I looked around I was living in Sydney with a severe modernist to whom the presence of a ukulele in the house would have been an outrage. With him it was Wagner or nothing. Even a string quartet or a solo piano was too minor. I had to put headphones on to listen to my funk tapes. It wasn't a dancing kind of marriage. How it flew past! Ejected, I scrambled to my feet in Bondi Junction Mall, dusted myself off, and got talking to a woman who was busking on a chunky little thing with a round body. She said it was called a pineapple uke and that her brother imported them from Hawaii. She gave me his phone number.

Oh, my Kamaka. It was so beautiful that I hated to put it away in its case. Even the wind wanted to play it. One day when I'd left it lying on the back of the couch and gone into the next room, the faintest, airiest twangling sound reached me. I ran back and found that a breeze coming up the hill from Bondi was puffing over the windowsill and drawing the hem of the calico curtain back and forth over the open strings.

Fast forward. I'm a grandmother, back in Melbourne where I belong. I've owned a ukulele for thirty years and I'm still a beginner. A uke is humble. It inspires in me no ambition, no duty or guilt. It's so low in the hierarchy of things that the bullying superego can't touch it. I play it only when I feel like it. After a particularly introverted winter, I got to the point where I could play 'All of Me', and 'I Will' (very slowly). But everything I learn I soon forget. I have to keep starting again. I can't pick, I can only strum, and I don't care. Sometimes I hold the uke on my knee while I'm reading the paper or waiting for the kettle to boil. I love it as I would any harmless little creature. I love to hear it whisper and hum.

Once in a while the money-making musicians in my family kindly call me when they're playing in the kitchen after tea, or at somebody's birthday party, or in the back shed that my sister calls her 'adobe hacienda'. There might be three or four ukes, a harmonica, a mandolin, a guitar. The chords aren't ones I know. The changes are too fast. Someone pushes the chart to me. I take a breath and throw myself into the river. No one can hear me, so it doesn't matter if I flounder. But if I don't panic, if I keep calmly swimming, sometimes I hit the current, and it carries me to the end of the song.

2015

Some Furniture

AT the turn of the millennium I reached the end of my masochism, and came home from Sydney with my tail between my legs. Single again. Tenants were still living in my Fitzroy house, and the one I rented for myself in Ascot Vale was too narrow for the table I'd had trucked down the Hume. I offered it to my niece. She turned up with a bloke in a ute and away they went. I stood in the bare room.

What can happen at the kitchen table when you haven't even got one?

A woman on her own can easily get into the habit of standing at the open fridge door and dining on a cold boiled potato. I was determined to be elegant in my solitude. But for lack of a table I had to eat off my knee, on the couch. The available space in the kitchen would take only a round table, and every round one I saw, in the crap shops I drifted through at Highpoint, had a hole drilled in the centre for an umbrella.

It chanced that a schoolfriend of my daughter's was married

to a woodworker. He came over, measured the spot, and returned in a couple of weeks with a perfect little creation in pale timber. It was so beautiful and so expensive that in my demoralised state I felt unworthy to sit at it. But I forced myself. I learnt to eat dainty salads off it, to nibble at fillets of fish steamed in ginger. This would be my single life.

A year later I took back my old house from the tenants. The kitchen was a large room. The little round table floated on its expanse of floor like an autumn leaf on a lake. How could something so lovely look so silly, so out of place? I rolled it into one of the bedrooms and drove down to the fashionable recycled timber shops on Johnston Street.

There I found a rectangular dining table of a suitable size. Until I bought my tiny round one, now superseded, I wouldn't have paid four figures for a table in a fit. But the sign said it was made of jarrah that had been salvaged from a demolished warehouse. Its dimensions were pleasing. It had slightly tapered legs and a glossy top, on which I could imagine setting out white crockery, cloth napkins, perhaps a vase of flowers if anything pretty ever blossomed again in my garden. For a moment I was puzzled by certain dark nail punctures that randomly pitted its surface. All the furniture in the shop seemed to have them. Maybe this was how recycled timber was supposed to look. Was the very purpose of this noble endeavour to preserve the traces of proletarian toil? Who was I, a self-pitying bohemian, to question this?

It looked all right in the kitchen. Its top gave off a warm, dark glow. One day, when I trudged in from work and dumped my red backpack on it, the two colours united in a fiery moment that made my mouth water. I looked out into the grassy yard. Perhaps a bird might alight, and emit a musical phrase. Something moved behind the lemon tree. I stepped over to the window and a hawk beat up into the air with a bald corpse hanging from its beak. I rushed outside. The grass behind the tree was thickly strewn with feathers.

I knew that I was in despair. The house was empty, too big for me to fill. All I could bring to it was an enormous, slow, bleak loneliness.

In a junk shop I found a shabby but surprisingly comfortable old sofa covered in gold brocade that was bleached almost to silver. When it was delivered I saw only its dated gentility; but then I tossed an equally ancient pink silk cushion on to it, and the pink and the faded gold sang to each other in quiet, tired voices. I saw that, living alone, one must play out one's domestic dramas through inanimate objects. Suddenly this did not seem so terrible.

But the man who had made me the little round table called in one afternoon. He stopped at the kitchen door and contemplated the recycled jarrah table without expression. Then he clicked his tongue and said, in a tone of reproachful pity, 'Oh, *Helen*.'

I supposed it was the nail holes. He refrained from a detailed critique and I brazened it out. After he left I got down on my haunches and had a look at the table's underside. I couldn't believe what I saw. The thing was cobbled together in the most shamelessly bodgie way. Random offcuts of raw pine, still sprouting ragged splinters, had been crudely jammed into its corners and stapled to brace it. No attempt had been made to hide the gross construction. It was blatant, insulting.

I tore off the jagged spikes with my bare hands, then pulled up a chair and sat at the table till the back garden got dark.

A married friend, whose house was notable for its quiet sophistication, came that week to visit me, bringing a bunch of flowers. She admired the table.

I said, 'Have a look underneath.'

She crawled under it, crouched there for a moment, then scrambled out and took her seat.

'Got vodka?'

I took the Absolut out of the freezer and found the shot glasses.

'Let's drink to your table,' she said.

'Don't tease me. I've been ripped off. I want revenge. I want a refund.'

'Look at it this way,' she said. 'It's stable, isn't it?'

It was.

'Is it the size you wanted?'

Perfect size.

'Fits the room?'

It did.

'Think about it,' she said. 'It's an image. Of you. Of all of us. It stands steady. It doesn't wobble. It's extremely serviceable. Okay, it's got those nail holes all over the top. But they're marks of experience. And when you look underneath, you see it's been pulled together out of whatever was to hand.'

Maybe it was the vodka, but after a moment's silence, I decided to take her analysis in the spirit in which it was meant. I arranged her flowers in a suitable vase, then we threw back another shot, leaned our elbows on the dark table's gleaming surface, and took up once more, at the point where we had left it last time, our endlessly interesting, fruitful and entertaining conversation.

2012

White Paint and Calico

THE night before I left my Fitzroy house forever, I sat down, exhausted after a day of packing and carrying, to watch *Supernanny*. I found myself consumed with disproportionate rage against the barbaric brothers she was trying to tame—three plain, fat-faced little slobs with prison haircuts and bare, flabby torsos. The parents were divided and ruled by these brats who swore, spat, sneered and smashed things, while their silent, obedient ten-year-old sister drifted about in the background, forgotten. I longed to spank the boys and slap their faces.

Any fool can see that at such a strained moment these characters were acting out aspects of myself, engaged in their eternal struggle for dominance or recognition. But at the time I thought I was only having a fit of the nameless emotion—testified to by everyone I've asked—that explodes in the heart and brain of a person who is about to move house.

'Oh, I hate the sorting, before you even start to pack,' said the former wife of a clergyman and veteran of many a vicarage. 'You're burrowing through cartons of stuff. You find something written on a piece of paper and suddenly you're on the floor in floods of tears, thinking about what you hoped for, and what you've lost. Every time you move you have to work through your whole *life*.'

A lawyer who has lived in more houses than there are years in her life said she held it all together by treasuring one small thing: her childhood teeth, in a matchbox. This year she turned forty, and threw them away.

A Japanese student told me that when she and her ex-husband were moved to Australia by his company, she opened the 200 boxes they had 'shipped and aired' and found she had packed every single thing they owned—'including a half-empty soy sauce bottle'.

In my storeroom, this time, I found half-a-dozen shoeboxes stuffed with photos I'd taken in the late 1980s, the ones that failed to make the cut for my album. I didn't chuck them out at the time because I was afraid if I did the people in them would die. The price I pay now for that superstition is having to endure how young we looked back then, my friends and I, though we were already in our late forties and thought ourselves ageing. Our faces were smaller, our skin fitted the skull more firmly, our heads were poised high on longer, more graceful necks. And, my God, is that Steve, when he was a Bible-bashing born-again? How could I have forgotten his lazy cowboy beauty? I ran out the back and crammed them into the bin, negs and all.

'When I was in labour with my first child,' said a teacher, 'I remember hearing myself yell: "I don't *want* this baby any more!" Moving house is like that—once you start, you have to keep going till it's done. And it doesn't matter how many people are there with you, all help is external, and beside the point. You're on your own.'

'Things improve,' said a musician from Bondi, 'once you stop expecting your friends to help you, and start paying people.'

'The removalists I hired,' said a young journalist at the Gin

Palace, 'were strangers to the point of being comical. They bumped the walls and broke things and sexually harassed me. They wouldn't lift things.'

The two blokes who came last month to shift my furniture struck a bolshie note as soon as they walked in. First they informed me that, though their boss had inspected it and given me a quote, there was no way they'd be able to fit all my stuff into the vast pantechnicon they had parked in front of my gate. Then, having filled me with such panic that I made the tactical blunder of calling the boss to complain, they began, in an extravagantly relaxed manner and refusing eye contact, to carry things out and arrange them roomily in the cavernous vehicle. Everything fitted, with space to spare.

So they sank the knife when it came to collecting my dead father's kitchen table from his empty house next door: apparently it was 'too heavy' and 'wouldn't fit through the door'.

'How do you think it got *in* here?' I said in a high-pitched voice.

'Musta took it apart and then reassembled it,' said one of them, fixing his gaze on the peeling lino. They closed up the truck and drove away, leaving me and the table standing in Dad's bare kitchen.

A week later, two men from my family tossed the table on to their flatbed truck and flipped it into my new house. They laughed. 'You were ripped off.'

Back in the big share houses of the '70s, when group dynamics were shaky and we were always having to split and start anew, people used to pride themselves on being able to polish off the move in a day. (*Bin all chutneys and mustards*.) The women, especially the single mothers, learnt how to set up a place at speed. You had to make things attractive and get the new household whirring along on its little rails so the kids could repose on a sense of order, and not be too sad about what they'd left behind.

Somebody told me that when Mother Teresa died all she left

behind was a bucket and a pair of sandals.

I read in his obituary that in 1936, when the late Sir Ronald Wilson was fourteen, the bank foreclosed on his family's home. Before the house was sold, young Ronald had to help bury his father's law library in the backyard.

A journalist fell in love and left his wife. Months later he went back to their house to pick up some things she had dumped for him outside the back door. Looking at the house, he realised he felt married to *it*, that it was his security, his only anchor. The place looked wild and out of control without his care. He wanted to clean it. He was suddenly very frightened: he would never have another like it. 'I started to whistle,' he told me, 'in case she was in there. I drove away angry. I wanted to turn back and stand by my dog's grave for a bit, but I was worried she might look out and see me standing there all sentimental.'

How many pets, carriers of helpless and unquestioning love, lie rotting under the backyards of the world, as houses change hands and again change hands?

'When you're a student,' said the teacher who had wanted her labour to stop, 'you move into a primitive, clapped-out house quite happily. You fix it up—white paint and calico—and you get on with your life. But when you're middle-aged you have a feeling that you should move into something better.'

I'm embarrassed that my new house is less substantial than the old one. Its walls feel fragile, insecurely grounded, not quite vertical. If I stumble, my elbow might go through the plaster. I imagine that people will step in the front door, take a look around and start to pity me. 'Well,' they say, trying to brighten me, 'at least you won't have to move again.' What—stay here *till I die*? In their concern they are consigning me to old age, to death. Is this why I have always kept moving? Because to stay in one place is deathly?

When I try to count the number of times I've moved, I start off confidently but conk out at about twenty-six. Everything starts to blur. My thoughts veer off to events and people connected to this house or that one, to the associated outrages and periods of fruitful calm. Old grievances, guilts and fits of self-righteousness fire up and smoulder again.

A Californian told me she had changed her address so often that she looked like 'a gun moll on the lam from the FBI'. Doesn't anybody stay in one place any more? Did they ever? Not according to Bruce Chatwin, who maintains in *The Songlines* that humans are supposed to be nomads—a theory that has always irritated me.

I heard somewhere of a woman who had moved forty times in ten years. After a short time in a place she would be filled with despair and overwhelmed by the urge to find a new house. Her dream was to have a home on wheels.

But how would it help, to live on wheels? Wouldn't her discomfort transfer itself to the landscape outside the caravan window? Wouldn't the sun be always slanting the wrong way, the trees casting a mistaken shade, the train roaring too close at night, the rubbish collected on the wrong day, the corner shop situated too far away and in the wrong direction?

A member of the original Circus Oz recalled her years on the road. 'At every stop,' she said, 'we would establish the caravans in a compound, and do the show in the big top each night. Then in a week we'd pull it all down again and move on. But the next time we parked the caravans, they'd be in a different relationship to each other. I was always very distressed until we got them hooked up to power and water. And the constant changes were very disturbing to the brain. By the end of the tour I would be so confused that I'd often mistake people I knew well for others in the group.'

Marcel Proust loved to write about the human need to subdue the unfamiliar and dull the pain it causes. He composed ironic hymns to 'habit! That skilful but slow-moving arranger who begins by letting our minds suffer for weeks on end in temporary quarters, but whom our minds are none the less only too happy to discover at last, for without it, reduced to their own devices, they would be powerless to make any room seem habitable.'

And yet those blissful Jungian dreams that everyone has, of finding in the house another room that you didn't know was there, high up under the roof, an extra storey, unused or neglected, but with more windows, sunshine pouring in, a glorious view, and more space than you've ever had before or imagined you deserved. You can't wait to sweep it out and furnish it and begin to inhabit it—to expand into it.

A house can be domineering, though. You have to get into the driver's seat. Sometimes it's only the light fittings that you need to subdue, but the task can seem beyond you. A screenwriter woke up on his first morning in a house he had bought, saw the ostentatious white and gold baubles dangling on long, marble-green rods from the bedroom ceiling, and began to weep: 'What have I done?'

There was something else too—he was grieving the death of his mother. The world won't slow down to give you time and space for moving house. It has to be done on top of everything else that's going on in your life. This must be why people like to recite the statistic that moving house is up there at the top of the stress list, after death and divorce—which, when you think about it, are just different forms of the same phenomenon.

When our mother died in her nursing home, and my father at eighty-nine moved into the cottage next door to me in Fitzroy, he bluntly refused to let his children sort through the stuff in the apartment that he was leaving. He made us pack the lot and bring it all along. At the time we were concentrating so hard on setting up his new house that we didn't notice how devastated he was by the move. He claimed as always to be feeling nothing, but roared a lot and waved his arms. His thin white hair, which he usually combed down flat with Listerine, stood up in a fluff, and his eyes were wild; but we just kept boring onward with the domestic tasks.

I hate now to think of that look on his face, both furious and desperately trusting, for he looked up at me the same way from his armchair on the summer morning, two years later, when I came in with my granddaughter to take him out for a coffee and he told me he'd stepped out of the shower and couldn't get his breath. By the time the sun had set that day, he was dead.

The house I've moved into is very similar in floor plan and orientation to the one I've left, so I set up my bed correspondingly, in the north-west corner. When I get into it I know where I am, and fall asleep at once. 'Bed is mother,' as a psychoanalyst suggested. And bed, if we're lucky enough to have one, is the centre of our personal universe, the safe point from which we let ourselves down into the shadow universe of sleep.

But now, when I wake each morning, though I'm horizontal and comfortable, though my feet are pointing the right way, I have at the same time a peculiar sensation that my shoulders are jammed up against the wall, that only the pressure of my back is keeping the house from sliding back to where a part of me still is, or thinks it should be: three kilometres closer to the city. I am holding the house westward of my former life by nothing but brute will. I can't even get my hand around the name of my new suburb when I fill in a form or write my address on a letter. It starts out dashingly then sags in the middle like a failed cake. And on a purely pragmatic level, I don't know how to get to anywhere else from here. Where do I find a decent coffee? Which way's the post office? What route do I take to cross the river? Where the hell *am* I?

This must be what it's like to be old. I feel flustered all the time. I can't seem to grasp things, or understand them, or concentrate. I need to be told ordinary facts over and over. I can't make decisions, or plan anything. Cooking is out of the question. The kitchen is full of unfamiliar outcrops: I can't move across it without hurting myself. Between the sink and the cutlery drawer, I smash my knee against a cupboard front and stand there snivelling with self-pity.

Anthropologists say that the house is an extension of the person, like an extra skin, or a shell: house, body and mind are in continuous interaction. A singer I know who loves to cook expressed it more gracefully. It took him months to find his ease in a new kitchen. 'What you have to re-establish,' he said, throwing out his arms and swinging his hips, 'is the dance of it.'

I've brought all the paintings and prints from my old house, but they're stacked on the floor with their faces to the wall. When I tip one or two of them back, to remind myself of what they are, I'm surprised and annoyed to find how many of them are full of darkness. A night road. A huge, gloomy cypress. A ferry moored at a night wharf. A moon shining on some black, rhythmic waves. And what daylight there is shows a paddock with one solitary gum standing forlornly in the middle. I don't want to bring that old darkness into this house.

But there's something shaming about undecorated walls and half-furnished rooms. Visitors go silent, then start offering advice: 'This hall's awfully bare. You need wall-hangings.' *Wall-hangings?* As if!

Now, a month later, I know where the return chute is at the library, the video shop. The stern Filipinos who run the post office have started to smile at me. I know the op shop doesn't open till eleven on Saturdays, that the motor that roars and roars at 10 p.m. at the bottom of the street is not some crazed hoon but the railway men mending the line. When the moon is full it blazes through my laundry window at bedtime, and into the bathroom at 4 a.m. I know that the café I like best is quieter at the end of the day than the library. Music plays there, but very low, and at each table sits a single person with a book or a newspaper or a mobile: absorbed, contained, content, with bowed head and motionless shoulders.

A solemn and very sensitive little boy moved with his family to Echuca. His parents had worked in advance to reproduce as exactly as they could the arrangements of his old bedroom in Melbourne. On moving day, when he first approached it, they held their breaths. He stood at the door in silence. Then he said in a soft, calm voice, '*Yes,*' and stepped forward into his room.

2005

Suburbia

IN the late 1970s I lived in Paris for a while with my daughter. She went to a local primary school where they served fresh artichokes for lunch but teachers rapped kids' knuckles with a ruler. I was trying to write my second book, on a grant from the Literature Board of the Australia Council. We rented a plain, ordinary, adequate apartment in an unglamorous part of the city, near the Porte de Saint-Ouen. Everyone thinks I must have loved living in Paris and had an exciting time. In fact I was paralysed with homesickness. I spoke fair French but I could not cut it socially. While my daughter was at school, I wrote all day in a library. I stayed home with her in the evenings. I desperately missed the big hippie households we had lived in, in North Fitzroy. I bought a pushbike, and chained it up in the dark, empty courtyard of the apartment building. The next morning I came down and found an anonymous note tied with string to the handlebar. It said, in old-fashioned curly handwriting, *Le cour n'est pas un garage.*

The Australian friend we shared the apartment with was gay. He was often out in the bars or cruising till dawn, busily catching AIDS, which he died of some years later, God rest him. The Frenchwoman who lived in the apartment below ours blamed us foreigners for any sound that pierced her slumber, and would open her window at 3 a.m. and shriek insults at us, though my daughter and I had been tucked up in our innocent beds since nine. One morning at the letterbox downstairs I got talking to the postie, a woman from Marseilles. We confessed our loneliness. She hated Parisians, she said. They were cold.

When I came back to Melbourne in 1980, and after I'd got used to the height of the sky and its glorious clarity, I looked for a place to live. I couldn't find a house to rent in the inner northern suburbs where I'd lived for years before I left. I borrowed a car and drove about in an ever-widening western arc. The suburb I stumbled on was Moonee Ponds. I had never been there before. In the minds of the intelligentsia, of course, it was a joke suburb, ever since Barry Humphries had unleashed on it his rage against the much more bourgeois eastern suburbs that had blighted his youth. The first thing that surprised me about Moonee Ponds was its beauty. Okay, Puckle Street, its main shopping street, was bald and hideous. But its old houses! Its park with a lake and a bandstand and elms and tall palm trees! Its quarter-acre blocks! Its backyards with lemon and fig trees!

A real estate agent directed me to a house he thought was about to be let, in a certain street off Mount Alexander Road. There I found an Italian bloke in his fifties called Dominic, up on a ladder in a freshly laundered white boiler suit, lovingly painting an empty three-bedroom weatherboard house. It had a shed, and a big grassy yard back and front. He and his family had moved out of it into a grander brick place round the corner. He wasn't at all sure he wanted to let his beloved old family house, especially to a woman. He was painfully attached to it. I practically tore it out of his hands. I even had to pretend to be married.

There was no estate agent involved in the deal. We had to take him the rent in cash, at his new house, every Saturday morning, and lay it discreetly on the dining room table while his wife served espresso coffee and almond biscuits. I witnessed his pain as his children left home before they married. It was the first time I had been exposed to a landlord's personal life.

This is how I first found myself living, as an adult, in what I realised was 'a suburb'—the very thing I had fled in 1961 when I left Geelong for Melbourne University, and had seen ever since as the emblem of everything I despised.

As my domestic life began to centre on Moonee Ponds, its name so unfairly a byword for the pretentious and the ridiculous, my feelings underwent a change. The beauty of those two words—Moonee Ponds—dawned on me. They made me think of a chain of quiet billabongs under a blurred moon. Many years later, I was in the back seat of a car in which Christopher Logue, the English poet and great translator of Homer, was being driven across town. We rolled down Brunswick Road and over the freeway, where the first sign to Moonee Ponds stood. From the front passenger seat rose a drawling, highly educated Pommy voice: 'I say…what's a *Moonee* Pond?' He had probably never heard of Edna Everage, and had no attitude towards the name of my erstwhile suburb, but the way he picked up the word in ironic tweezers made me want to seize him from my seat in the back and garrotte him.

Last summer I was spending a week with my sister at a health farm outside Penrith. I should mention that I was fasting. I turned on the TV in my room and found in progress a documentary about Barry Humphries. It showed black-and-white footage from the 1950s: a man in tightly rolled up shirtsleeves polishing his new FJ Holden with exaggeratedly vigorous arm movements; a bunch of unsmiling middle-aged women in horn-rimmed spectacles and hats like meringues. These people were offered to us viewers for our mockery. But in the 1950s I was a provincial Australian schoolgirl. I *lived* back then, in a suburb of Geelong. In that documentary footage I saw nothing to sneer at. What struck me was the man's cheerful pride and energy. I saw the women's shyness, their anxiety about being no longer young, their uncertainty about whether they would be considered fashionable or attractive; and my heart cracked.

Those mocked people in Moonee Ponds or Manifold Heights or Newtown—didn't they too love and hope and work and suffer and try to help each other, and die? I wanted to speak up, now that it's too late, for my parents, and for my parents' friends—those shy, modest, public-spirited people. On weekends they built themselves a bowling green with their bare hands. On Saturday nights they did ballroom dancing in their clubhouse to a daggy amateur band. The fathers twirled us clumsy girls around in our layered petticoats and big white shoes. These people were kind to their neighbours' children. They were proud of us and showed us their affection. They gave us a glass of lemon cordial and a biscuit after school, and let us play 'Chopsticks' and 'Heart and Soul' on their piano for hours without complaining. They weren't related to us but we called them all Auntie and Uncle. They arrived at each other's barbecues freshly dressed and smiling, carrying a plate of shortbread biscuits, or a bowl of salad covered with a damp tea towel. The women ran up cotton frocks on sewing machines. The men went fishing and brought home huge feasts of flounder. They worked hard and tried to live decently. In old age, long after the families had scattered all over the map, the survivors turned up faithfully at funerals.

I'm ashamed now of my bohemian contempt for the suburbs of my childhood, of my longing to be sophisticated. In the 1990s I lived in Sydney, in Elizabeth Bay, a part of town full of flats and cool cafés, but empty of children; then on the border of Bellevue Hill and Bondi Junction, to me a place of loneliness and strange humiliation, where the young residents of my apartment building would sail through the lobby each morning without even granting the fact of their neighbours' existence.

In 2000 I came back to Melbourne and rented a house in the suburb of Ascot Vale. My daughter had found it for me: she chose it because it was right opposite a primary school. Working in my kitchen I would stop still and listen to the high, long, sweet, wordless cry that rises from children at play.

Now, as a grandmother, I live in a suburb that to some of my friends is off the beaten track. To get *this far west* they have to work their way round *obstacles*: the cemetery and the university, the untracked wastes of Royal Park. They have to pass the zoo. They even have to *cross the freeway*.

I met my neighbours en masse one night after dinner, when some kids from the flats crashed a stolen car through the fence at the bottom of our street and down the bank of the railway line. Everybody rushed out to see. People introduced themselves; they welcomed me. A woman ran inside for a blanket and wrapped it round the shoulders of the driver, whose teeth were chattering with shock. When the cops turned up, an officious young policewoman told us to go back to our homes. My neighbours bristled. We all stood closer together. One bloke muttered, 'I'm going to bring out my barbecue.' It was our street, and we weren't going inside till we were good and ready.

My next-door neighbour Chris comes out to cut her nature strip, sees that mine is bedraggled, and runs her mower across it as a matter of course, without thinking of it as a favour or asking for appreciation. Her children's white rabbit sneaks through a hole in the side fence and spends leisurely afternoons in my backyard. My grandchildren's unloved guinea pig, Guadalupe, fled under the fence into Chris's yard; a week or so later Chris let us know that it was now male, and its name was Philip. We stand out the front under the plane trees talking about chooks and the return of the foxes. We talk about compost. I begin to see that suburbia might be merely another term for *dirt*, or *children*, or *vegetation*.

A few years ago the brilliantly original and eccentric Victorian writer Gerald Murnane won the Melbourne Prize for Literature. It's a big prize, and half of it is supposed to be spent on overseas travel. When Murnane heard he'd been short-listed, he told the committee to withdraw his name, since he had never left the country and was resolutely opposed to the idea of doing so. The committee had the sense to relax the travel clause and award him the prize. In his acceptance speech he explained his refusal to go abroad, and outlined his simple plan for travel *within* Australia: he was going to visit all the houses in Melbourne that he had ever lived in.

Then he tilted back his head, closed his eyes, and recited a long list of all his former addresses in the suburbs of Melbourne: plainly named streets in obscure, lower-middle-class suburbs that no one ever goes to or hears about in the news. And as he reeled them off, by heart, without hesitation, in chronological order, we all held our breath, with tears in our eyes, because we knew that he was reciting a splendid and mysterious poem. It was a naming of parts of the mighty machine that had created the imaginative world of an artist. And when he finished, and opened his eyes, the place went up in a roar of joy.

2011

PART TWO

Notes from a Brief Friendship

Dear Mrs Dunkley

IN 1952, when I was nine and my name was Helen Ford, I came from Ocean Grove State School, where the teachers were kindly country people, to a private girls' school in Geelong. I was put into your grade five class.

You were very thin, with short black hair and hands that trembled. You wore heels, a black calf-length skirt and a black jacket with a nipped-in waist.

We had Arthur Mee's Children's Encyclopedia at home, and I thought I was pretty good at General Knowledge.

'In what year was the Great Plague of London?'

Up flew my hand. '1665.'

You stared at me. 'I *beg* your pardon?' You mimicked my flat, nasal, state school accent. You corrected it. You humiliated me. I became such a blusher that other kids would call out, 'Hey Fordie! What colour's red?'

I was weak at arithmetic. On such weakness you had no mercy. 'Stand up, you great MOON CALF.' You made us queue at your table to show you our hopelessly scratched-out and blotted exercise books. Close up you emitted a faint and terrifying odour: a medicinal sort of perfume. On your lapel twinkled a sinister marcasite brooch.

Every morning, first thing after the bell, you would write in chalk on the blackboard the numerals of the clock face, then take the long wooden pointer and touch the figures, one by one, in random order, in a slow, inexorable rhythm. We had to add them silently in our heads, and have the answer ready when you stopped. The name of this daily practice was THE DIGIT RING.

You made us keep our hands on the desks so we couldn't count on our fingers, but I learnt to make my movements too small to be visible: to this day I can add up on my fingers like lightning. But the psychic cost of the digit ring was high. My mother had to wake me from nightmares. 'You were calling out in your sleep,' she'd say. 'You were screaming out "The digit ring! The digit ring!" What on earth,' she asked innocently, '*is* a digit ring?'

Dear Mrs Dunkley. You taught us not only arithmetic. One day, making us all sick with shame that our mothers had neglected their duties, you taught grade five to darn a sock. You taught us to spell, and how to write a proper letter: the address, the date, the courteous salutation, the correct layout of the page, the formal signing off. But most crucially, you taught us grammar and syntax. On the blackboard you drew up meticulous columns, and introduced us to Parts of Speech, Parsing, Analysis. You showed us how to take a sentence apart, identify its components, and fit them back together with a fresh understanding of the way they worked.

One day you listed the functions of the adverb. You said, 'An adverb can modify an adjective.' Until that moment I had known only that adverbs modified verbs: *they laughed loudly; merrily we roll along.* I knew I was supposed to be scratching away with my dip pen, copying the list into my exercise book, but I was so excited by this new idea that I put up my hand and said, 'Mrs Dunkley, how can an adverb modify an adjective?'

You paused, up there in front of the board with the pointer in your hand. My cheeks were just about to start burning when I saw on your face a mysterious thing. It was a tiny, crooked smile. You looked at me for a long moment—a slow, careful, serious look. You looked at me, and, for the first time, I knew that you had seen me.

'Here's an example,' you said, in an almost intimate tone. '*The wind was terribly cold.*'

I got it, and you saw me get it. Then your face snapped shut.

I never lost my terror of you, nor you your savage contempt. But if arithmetic lessons continued to be a hell of failure and derision, your English classes were a paradise of branching and blossoming knowledge.

Many years later, dear Mrs Dunkley, when I had turned you into an entertaining ogre from my childhood whose antics made people laugh and shudder, when I had published four books and felt at last that I could call myself a writer, I had a dream about you. In this dream I walked along the sandstone veranda of the school where you had taught me, and looked in through the French doors of the staffroom. Instead of the long tables at which the teachers of my childhood used to sit, marking exercise books and inventing horrible tests and exams, I saw a bizarre and miraculous scene.

I saw you, Mrs Dunkley, moving in slow motion across the staffroom—but instead of your grim black 1940s wool suit, you were dressed in a jacket made of some wondrously tender and flexible material, like suede or buckskin, in soft, unstable colours that streamed off you into the air in wavy bands and ribbons and garlands, so that as you walked you drew along behind you a thick, smudged rainbow trail.

In 1996 I described this dream in the introduction to a collection of my essays. A few months after the book came out, I received a letter from a stranger. She had enjoyed my book, she said, particularly the introduction. She enclosed a photo that she thought I might like to see.

The photo shows a woman and a teenage girl standing in front of a leafy tree, in a suburban backyard. It's an amateurish black-and-white snap of a mother and daughter: it cuts off both subjects at the ankles. The girl is dressed in a gingham school uniform. Her haircut places the picture in about 1960. She is slightly taller than the woman, and is looking at the camera with the corners of her mouth drawn back into her cheeks; but her eyes are not smiling; they are wary and guarded.

The woman in the photo is in her late forties. She has short, dark, wavy hair combed back off her forehead. Her brows are dark and level, her nose thin, her lips firmly closed in an expression of bitter constraint. Deep, hard lines bracket her mouth. She's wearing a straight black skirt and a black cardigan undone to show a neat white blouse buttoned to the neck. Her hands are hanging by her sides.

I showed the photo to my husband. 'What enormous hands!' he said.

I knew your hands, Mrs Dunkley. Not that they ever touched me, but I recall them as thin and sinewy and fierce looking, with purplish skin that seemed fragile. They quivered, in 1952, with what I thought was rage, as you skimmed your scornful pencil-point down my wonky long divisions and multiplications.

'My mother,' wrote the stranger in her letter, 'was an alcoholic.'

I thought I knew you, Mrs Dunkley. I thought that by writing about you I had tamed you and made you a part of me. But when I looked at that photo, I felt as if I'd walked into a strange room at night, and something imperfectly familiar had turned to me in the dark. The real Mrs Dunkley shifted out from under the grid of my creation, and I saw you at last, my teacher: an intense, damaged, dreadfully unhappy woman, only just holding on, fronting up to the school each morning, buttoned into your black clothes, savagely impatient, craving, suffering: a lost soul.

Dear Mrs Dunkley. You're long gone, and I'm nearly seventy. But, oh, I wish you weren't dead. I've got some things here that I wouldn't be ashamed to show you. And I've got something I want to say. I would like to thank you. It's probably what you would have called *hyperbole*, but, Mrs Dunkley, you taught me everything I know. Other teachers, later, consolidated it. But you were the one who laid the groundwork. You showed me the glory and the power of an English sentence and the skills I would need to build one. You put into my hands the tools for the job.

Dear Mrs Dunkley. I know that your first name was Grace; I hope you found some, in the end. Please accept, in whatever afterlife you earned or were vouchsafed, the enduring love, the sincere respect, and the eternal gratitude of your Great Moon Calf, Helen.

2011

Eight Views of Tim Winton

one

The first time I clapped eyes on the physical Tim Winton was in 1982. I'd reviewed his novel *An Open Swimmer* in the *National Times*, one of those publications 'over east' which Tim regarded with the dark suspicion of the dyed-in-the-wool West Australian.

Soon after this, I was one of the east-coast guests, along with David Marr and Blanche d'Alpuget, at a writers' weekend in Fremantle. On the plane out Blanche befriended me. I was impressed by her negative ion generator, her neat little cream suit and her work-in-progress, a biography of Bob Hawke. She and I were given adjoining rooms at the hotel. Early on the first morning she called me in. Charming, blonde, glamorous, she gave a brilliant demonstration of how to manage a laden breakfast tray while reclining against voluptuous movie-star pillows. I trudged to the day's session, Bertha Bigfoot from Geelong.

From the stage I scanned the audience. One young man's head

was tilted in a way I'd seen in a photo somewhere. A fall of straight shiny brown hair. An expression of earnest concentration on an egg-smooth, freckled face. And he was staring at *me*. Hell, wasn't that Winton? Stabbed with panic, I scoured my memory for what I'd said in the review. I liked the novel and had said so; but from the lofty eminence of a minimalist who'd published fully two books, I'd drawn attention to what I saw as his overworked metaphors: a character doesn't just take a mouthful of beer, for example, but *nudges the bitter foam*. Oh, Gawd. I dreaded the tea-break. And yet I knew I'd be more at home with this provincial long hair than with the suave political journalists from Sydney.

two

Cut to the state of having known each other forever. It's an unlikely friendship—I'm almost as old as his mother. That day at Fremantle was the start of a long conversation. Thick envelopes arrived from Perth, neatly addressed in his sloping, clear, best-writer-grade-six hand, which is still the same today. Were the letters about what he was reading and writing, what vegetables they were planting, what fish they were catching and eating? He and Denise had just got married. They'd known each other since primary school. They were very happy. Secretly, in my inner-city, divorced feminist way, I thought what they'd done was *very dangerous*. When I eventually got to visit their house, I looked at their wedding photos on the mantelpiece and noticed once again that earnest expression of Tim's. He stood behind Denise with his arms round her, and glared into the camera, his eyes almost crossing with intensity. *I am her husband: she is my wife.* Denise looked calm and sweet and funny. She was doing nursing, back then. On night shifts she used to write me quietly delirious letters on lined lecture pads and sign them Nurse Pam. Who the hell was Nurse

Pam? A cartoon character? Our friendship was constructed on a grid of these references. And on jokes about farting, bums and general scatology, which are a Winton family tradition.

three

In 1984 Jesse, the first of the Wintons' kids, was born. The planned home birth deteriorated into trauma and crisis. Along with the baby-and-mother photos, Tim sent me a picture of himself, bulging-eyed, staggering in a blood-stained boiler suit along the bare corridor of a hospital. *I am a father*. That year I was writer-in-residence at the University of Western Australia and lived in Perth for nine weeks. I hurried to their house and was handed the baby to hold. Happily I strolled about the neat living room, murmuring to this tiny Jesse, pulling rank, fancying myself as an *experienced mother*. Then something disturbed the baby and he began to wriggle, to whimper, to cry and then to squall. I rushed to find Tim in the other room and held out the bundle to him. He kept his hands in his pockets and grinned at me in an infuriating way. 'No,' he said. '*You* do it.' So I had to, and I did.

four

I shared a house in Melbourne, in the mid-'80s, with a recently 'saved' Christian who used to harangue me about Jesus at the drop of a hat. Tim came to stay a night or two. The saved one was very keen to meet Tim, and had planned a weighty theological discussion: the big black Bible was on the dining room table while we drank our tea and ate our cake. I couldn't face it, and went for a walk round the big park. When I got home an hour later, Tim and the Bible were still at the table. 'Where is he?' 'Gone upstairs for a nap, I think.' 'What happened?'

'Oh…we talked. And in the end I said to him, "Why don't you give the book a rest? Why don't you let your life be your witness?"'

five

I envied Tim his large, free-rolling, open-air-and-water imagination. I envied him when we got on a plane together and the hostess asked him for his autograph. I got cranky with him when he spurned the European writers I revered and clung to regional Americans I'd never heard of. I sent him a jubilant letter: 'Hey! I've just written a 200-word sentence which is syntactically perfect!' 'I couldn't care less,' he replied, 'about that sort of shit.' He was cranky with me when he published *Cloudstreet* and I wouldn't read it until I'd finished my try at a book about a house, *Cosmo Cosmolino*. I was jealous because everybody loved his book and nobody loved mine. I managed to pick a couple of squabbles. He seemed baffled by this and for a while half-heartedly played the part I gave him in my neurotic inner-city drama of 'friendship', until we both got bored with it and went back to our ordinary cheerful correspondence.

six

When my third husband and I went to stay with Tim and Denise at their fibro shack up the coast from Perth, they served meals of such oceanic munificence that we could not cope. What they thought of as a first course would have kept us going, in our etiolated Sydney existence, for days. Our stomachs were not big enough for their generosity. They looked at us, puzzled, over the mounds of fishy splendour in the centre of the table. They had the strong physical energy of a country life: three kids, a dog, a guitar, a fishing boat. We lived in our heads: self-starved, over-disciplined. And it showed.

seven

Tim came east on a promotion tour and asked if he could go to church with me one Sunday morning. That day we sang the eighteenth-century hymn that goes:

> Long my imprison'd spirit lay
> Fast bound in sin and nature's night
> Thine eye diffus'd a quick'ning ray
> I woke. The dungeon flam'd with light
> My chains fell off, my heart was free
> I rose, went forth and follow'd thee.

At the repetition of the words *My chains fell off* we glanced at each other and started to laugh. Later, we knelt side by side at the communion rail. Usually, when the priest offers you the chalice and says 'The blood of Christ', you reply 'Amen'. I still don't know if I dreamt this, but when Tim took the chalice and heard the formal words, he answered, 'Thanks, mate.'

eight

Once, when I was staying at the Wintons' place, Denise and I were mucking around in the kitchen, cooking the dinner. Tim rushed in with news: his agent had phoned him to say that a very handsome offer for the film rights to one of his novels had come in from a famous American company. But Tim had signed a local film contract for the same book only the day before. He lurched about the kitchen hitting cupboard doors with his flat palms, cursing and bewailing his luck. I began to commiserate. Denise worked on in silence while the two writers luxuriously whinged. Then she cut across us in a sharp, clear, level voice, matching the rhythm of her words to her physical movements: '*Denise* puts the *roast* in the *oven*. *LIFE. GOES. ON.*' She slammed the oven door. We stopped talking. She opened a bottle and poured three glasses. We drank them. And life did just as she said.

1999

Notes from a Brief Friendship

WHEN I was invited to write a cover line for Jacob Rosenberg's second book of memoir, *Sunrise West*, I knew only that his first memoir, *East of Time*, had won several prizes and was highly thought of; so I promised the endorsement, sight unseen, and sat down, pencil in hand, to read both volumes.

The narrator I found there was likeable, but his style at first was not congenial to me—a heightened rhetoric, dialogue of ornate wryness, a taste for the ringing phrase. My initial reservation about his technique must have been an unconscious attempt to shield myself from the nub of the story he had to tell, for when it came I was not prepared for the sickening jolt of his family's arrival and immediate destruction at Birkenau. *Within the blink of an eye I became bestially free... I am not trying to explain. There is nothing to elucidate.*

Since I was a teenager I have read many books about the Nazis' attempts to destroy the Jews, but no matter how often or with what close attention I contemplate accounts of these horrible crimes and sufferings, I have never been able to hold steady their details in my head. Again, with Jacob Rosenberg's books, I read with heart in mouth, but a protective amnesia blotted out what my eyes had just travelled across. To fix the murdered Jewish children's ages in my mind I would stand them beside a mental picture of my grandchildren, then shrink in panic from that manoeuvre. Whenever Rosenberg put a date to some unspeakable barbarity of the early 1940s, I would be stopped in my tracks by the fact that in the same year my young mother was wheeling me in my pram along the clean new streets of suburban Geelong, unmolested, ignorant of terror, naively privileged to have been born in the very land to which Jacob and his wife, Esther, exhausted, bereft and brutalised, would stagger in 1948—which he describes in his book as 'an amazingly peaceful world soaked in sun'. How was it possible that these wild extremes were taking place at the same moment? Would I ever be able to understand or grasp this phenomenon?

Yet I found that Jacob Rosenberg wrote with a kind of mercy for the reader. He drew with fierce strokes a scene of the most savage brutality, and then relaxed into a vignette of human interaction tinged with unexpected sweetness and even humour.

He was a deft sketcher of physical appearance, with a knowing eye for what people's clothes, and the way they wear them, could reveal: *a smallish condescending man who always wore a white shirt with a black tattered bow tie.* Sometimes he took a fleeting pleasure in an item of clothing: *a silky white shirt*, perhaps, *trimmed with an emerald tie.* His attitudes towards religious faith and the idea of God were undogmatic, and beautifully complex: when he wrote about soup, for example, he made clear not only its preciousness to the physically starving, but also its sacramental meaning and value. In fact, I found that he was impressively in command of something I have heard a Christian call *the sacrament of whatever's necessary.*

I wrote a humbled sentence for the book cover and sent it to the publisher.

Soon Jacob Rosenberg himself phoned to thank me. He was a man in his eighties, twenty years my senior, with delicate manners and a voice with a smile in it, tremulous, a little bit reedy. He would like to take me to lunch. Would I suggest a restaurant? I proposed the European in Spring Street, opposite the Parliament.

He turned out to be a small, slight man, in glasses, with eyes that peeped brightly over their frames. His hair grew in white puffs above his ears. His English was very fluent, with a strong accent.

The food at the European that day was delicious and Jacob seemed pleased by it; but our table was tiny and ill-placed, and the noise level close to unbearable: we sat there for an hour yelling at each other. This was not what I had envisaged. Still, we communicated. He told me that writing was the only way he could make sense of the world. His granddaughter, he said, was a fan of my work. I suspected that he had not read any of it himself, and that if he had, it would not have appealed to him. This made me feel relaxed and free: relieved that I would not be obliged to account for myself. He had brought me, as a gift, one of his earlier books, *Lives and Embers*. The stories in it, he said, were 'parables, stripped of detail, but rather sentimental'. He asked me to launch *Sunrise West*. I said I would be honoured. Rain began to fall while we were inside the restaurant, so heavily that we ordered another glass of mineral water, another pot of tea, rather than leave the building and get drenched. A man of my father's generation, Jacob picked up the tab with a confident swoop.

On the tram home I opened *Lives and Embers*, with its brown-tinged, almost comically beautiful Modigliani double portrait on the cover. I riffled the pages at random and my eye fell on this: *It was in the early days of September 1944 that I saw my sister Pola for the last time. Her head had been shaved. She wore a loose white shift that clung to her swollen legs. She was stretched out on the electric fence at Auschwitz, finally at rest.* Breathless, I turned back to the title page and found that he had written there, in a neat, foreign hand, *To dear Helen*.

Next time we met, we tried the Windsor Hotel, where the floor was carpeted and diners could converse; I used to meet my father there after my mother died. Jacob and I ate grills with salad. His eyes were very bright and warm behind the spectacles. He tilted his head while he listened and thought. He told me a thrilling story about the time when his daughter Marcia, working for Doubleday in New York, needed a special outfit for an occasion she was to attend in the company of Jackie Onassis, who had been very supportive of her; he had designed and made, in record time, a beautiful velvet suit 'with a jabot. Do you know *jabot*?' He made an eloquent one-handed gesture at his throat and I got the picture.

Although Jacob appeared to enjoy the Windsor, I felt again that we had not found the right venue. A few months later he took the matter of the restaurant into his own hands. We would meet at an Italian place on Toorak Road in South Yarra. This was off my patch. I took the train. He had told me the address, but tramp up and down as I might, I couldn't find it. At last I spotted a figure in a raincoat on the other side of the street, waving patiently. He had given me an odd number instead of an even. When I hurried across the tramline and teased him about his error, he seemed annoyed with me for a moment, frowned, and looked away. This too reminded me fondly of my father.

The owner of the Italian bistro greeted Jacob with a respectful affection that made him relax and glow: he was known here, a beloved patron. I too was at ease in this old-style restaurant, with its dark timbers and enormous menu and middle-aged waiters in long aprons. We ventured a glass of wine.

He brought out of his briefcase a copy of *Sunrise West*, the new book I was to launch, and passed it across the table. It was a paperback from Brandl & Schlesinger, like all their books elegantly and powerfully designed. On the cover was a black-and-white shot of a young couple in heavy overcoats, striding towards the camera, both with thick dark wavy hair swept back handsomely from their foreheads. Their expressions were the unposed ones of people caught unawares on a pavement by a 1940s street photographer.

'It's you! With your wife?'

'Yes, with Esther, in Marseilles,' he said, 'in 1948, just before we left for Australia.'

'I thought Marseilles was a warm place. Why those big leather gloves? Look—the man behind you is only wearing a light suit.'

'It was the iceblocks I had to carry,' he said with a shrug. 'After that my hands never got warm.'

He was happy today, he said, because he had spent the morning working on his new book, a novel, and had written a sentence that he was pleased with: *Youth is like a diamond, unaware of its own brilliance.* We raised a glass to youth and its innocent shine.

Jacob was very friendly. I liked him and I think he liked me. And yet we were always slightly awkward with each other. Our social styles did not easily mesh. When our conversation moved in a direction he was not comfortable with—if I indulged in idle psychologising, or made a crack aimed at provoking light laughter—he gently drew me back on to his turf by offering a philosophical generalisation, a piece of wisdom about life or literature. I had known other male writers, particularly ones who worshipped at European cultural shrines, who had this habit. I was aware that Jacob was friendly with certain Australian novelists, poets and philosophers who were men: that this was the milieu in which he most liked to move. He was an old man, no doubt an autodidact—he wrote that Auschwitz was his university—and his style was to express himself in well-considered, hard-won nuggets of thought. He would lay them down on the cloth between us, peering up at me on an angle with his bright eyes; and I, the beneficiary of a university education that I had been too lazy to take advantage of, would sit there gazing at them helplessly. I have never been any good at generalising, or at responding to other people's philosophical insights. Jacob was seeking literary companionship, but I was not able to provide it, or not as he conceived it. The gulf that separated us, I think, was the one that lies between those who love chess and those who grasp neither its rules nor its purpose.

Some of his men friends had repeated to me the statements of deep, stoical bleakness that he had made to them. He never spoke that way to me. Perhaps he felt that I was naïve, that he ought to spare me the worst of what his experiences had taught him.

Re-reading a random page of *Sunrise West* on my way home from the South Yarra restaurant that day, I came upon this lovely three-sentence account of exhausted prisoners crossing at last into Italy: *We moved out by moonlight, after being transferred to a goods train once again. The night was warm and the shutters of our carriage were left wide open. We rushed through a pastoral world unknown to me.*

Yes—when the chips were down, when his storytelling voice breathed freely and I heard it without defence, my respect and affection for him were unconstrained.

After the launch of *Sunrise West*, at which he spoke with a gracious simplicity and with an impressive mastery of the pause, and after the pleasant celebration later at the Rosenbergs' house, where he and his family welcomed me with warm friendliness, I hardly saw Jacob again. We lived on opposite sides of the city, and the city seemed to have become dispiritingly wide. Once or twice we spoke cheerfully on the phone. Work was his chief preoccupation and joy. He was close to finishing his novel. He sounded somewhat breathless. The word *angina* was mentioned.

In a little more than a year, Alex Miller called one morning to tell me that Jacob had died of a heart attack, on the eve of the day a big publisher had intended to call him with an offer for his just-finished novel *The Hollow Tree*.

I drove out to Springvale for his funeral. The service was conducted in the style at which Jews excel: deeply satisfying in its formality, tender in the beauty of its readings and tributes.

Two days later, after timidly attending the minyan, I stepped out his front gate and headed for my car. It was almost dusk and the sky was full of dramatic, dark clouds. It struck me that Jacob would never again walk along his own street, or see with gladness the calm leafy trees of his suburb. The brevity and shyness of our friendship made me feel suddenly weak with sadness.

Soon after Jacob's death, Radio National's Book Show replayed an old interview with him. 'Suffering is so singular an art,' he said, in his reedy, softly humorous voice; and 'I believe that nothing is lost in the universe, somehow.'

Reading his memoirs again, now, I am flooded by the memory of a dream I had, many years before I met Jacob. On the lip of an abyss roaring with dark wind stood a tiny bush that bore an intensely red flower. The bush grew right on the very edge of nothingness, and yet somehow its roots were holding. It had a grip that no wind could disturb; it thrived there, all on its own, this modest little plant, and while the abyss yawned beside it, it went on bravely, doggedly flowering.

2011

From Frogmore, Victoria

LAST winter on a plane to the Mildura Writers' Festival I happened to sit next to Raimond Gaita. Like many people who have read his memoir *Romulus, My Father*, I felt I knew him better than I actually do. I asked him if it was true that Eric Bana was going to play Romulus in the movie adaptation that I'd heard Richard Roxburgh was directing. He opened his laptop and showed me some stills: the replica of Frogmore, the crumbling weatherboard shack of his childhood; Bana riding a motorbike with a plaster cast on his leg; a rangy boy running and laughing in a dusty yard. The movie-Raimond looked about nine. He had a face so open that it hurt to look at it.

'His name,' said Gaita, 'is Kodi Smit-McPhee.'

'Did you go to the shoot?'

'I kept away,' he said. 'I thought my presence might throw him off. He might think, Is *this* what's ahead for me?' He gave a small laugh. 'But near the end I went. Richard introduced us. We stood and looked at each other. We both cried. He said, "I've lived your life for the last three months." And then for an hour he wouldn't leave my side.'

There's a brief scene, quite early in the movie, in which Raimond is mooching along a street and sees a teenage girl dancing wildly to a record on her front porch. He calls out and asks her the name of the singer. She tells him it's Jerry Lee Lewis, from Ferriday, Louisiana. 'And who are you, when you're at home?' she asks coldly. The screen fills with the boy's eager, unbearably smiling and undefended face. 'I'm Raimond Gaita,' he says, 'from Frogmore, Victoria!'

At that moment a faint sound rustled through the first preview audience: part laughter, part sigh. Gaita was in the cinema that evening. I wondered how he would sit through this new telling of his childhood, a version over which he'd had little or no control.

It's a story of suffering: obsessive love, sexual betrayal and jealousy; abandonment of small children; violence, madness and despair; two suicides; repeated acts of forgiveness and loyalty that are nothing short of heroic. Yet threaded through all this is the miraculous blossoming of a child's intellect.

The book changed the quality of the literary air in this country. People often take an unusually emotional tone when they speak about it, as if it had performed for them the function that Franz Kafka demanded: 'A book must be the axe for the frozen sea within us.' Reading it, with its stiff, passionate dignity and its moral demands, can smash open a reader's own blocked-off sorrows. Out they rush to meet those that the book relates.

For a movie to be drawn from this memoir, the tale would have had to be taken apart, and the pieces picked up off the floor and compressed into a new configuration, without the one element that holds it all together on the page, makes sense of it, and redeems it: Gaita's unique narrating voice.

It's an intellectual's voice, a philosopher's, fastidious, restrained, wary. It's wonderfully serious, and terrified of being sentimental. At times it quivers with a suppressed, righteous anger. It can be disdainful, lofty to the point of chilliness, as when he refines and yet again refines his father's beliefs and motives, holding them away defensively from what he imagines the reader might lazily suppose them to have been: no, it wasn't *this*, he keeps insisting—it was *that*.

And then, suddenly, it will relax and open out into an image of sensuous joy: 'roads especially dusted to match the high summer-coloured grasses'; or a blunt domestic fact: 'the chickens came into the house and shat in it'; or a quiet statement of breathtaking humility: 'I know what a good workman is; I know what an honest man is; I know what friendship is; I know because I remember these things in the person of my father, in the person of his friend Hora, and in the example of their friendship.'

How can film match this striding, all-creating, all-encompassing thing, the voice?

I saw Gaita emerge into the lobby after the preview. He looked vague, and numb. I would have liked to make a comradely gesture, but I didn't understand what the movie was doing to me, so I bolted for the train. I cried all the way home, and on and off for days afterwards.

'You can't imagine,' shouts Gaita over the rattling of his loose-jointed old ute, 'how much more beautiful it is round here when there's *grass*.'

But up here near Baringhup in Central Victoria, where Gaita is showing me the sites of his childhood story, the grass is gone. Drought has stripped the ground and worn its surface to a grey-brown velvet. The paddocks are infested with a plague of wheel cactus—nasty, plate-shaped pads of pale green, fringed with sparse hairy spines.

'The stuff's out of control,' says Gaita. 'And it can grow straight out of a rock.'

We park and set out on foot towards the granite boulders among which Romulus Gaita's friend Vacek, a harmless hermit, made himself a fortress. I spot a baby cactus sprouting insolently from a dinted stone.

'Eww, gross,' I say. 'It *is* growing out of bare rock.'

'You thought it was mere hyperbole, didn't you,' says Gaita.

This is the first time I've ever heard anyone use the phrase 'mere hyperbole' in conversation. Before I can remark on this, which I'm not at all sure I'm going to, we fetch up against the first boulder.

Despite his grand philosopher's head with its white hair and glasses, Gaita is a small, agile fellow, a rock climber from way back. Up he goes, smooth as a lizard. He leans down to me.

'Get your toe in there, see?'

I obey. He reaches down and grabs my hand.

'Now,' he says, 'you just *run* up it.'

Somehow my other foot gains a purchase on the granite. He lets go my hand and suddenly I'm running. I bound up the damn thing. In four light springs I'm standing on its flat top, not even out of breath. I glow with relief. Gaita is not the sort of person before whom one would like to appear foolish, or gutless; and I'm not yet sure why.

These austere volcanic plains, across which a vast, leisurely body of air is forever passing, have carried for Gaita since childhood an unabashedly transcendental meaning.

'I needed the filmmakers,' he shouts as the ute rattles along, 'to understand how utterly fundamental to the story the landscape was. They saw it at all hours of the day and night—they fell in love with it. The first time Nick Drake [the British poet who wrote the screenplay] came to Baringhup, I drove him along this road. It was a bit later in the day. And when we came round this bend, the light over there was thick gold.'

Today the sky is partly clouded. The land is grey, grey, grey, racked and bare. But its bones are glorious—low contours under colossal, purifying skies.

'Now,' he yells, 'you're about to see what drought *really* is.'

We bounce over a rise and down the side of a large, lumpy, broad, grey valley a couple of kilometres wide. Right at the bottom lies a small, narrow body of water, sausage-shaped and murky. Its steely surface riffles in the wind. Gaita pulls off the track and stops. I look round vaguely. There's something odd about this place, something not quite natural.

'This is where Hora and I used to take the boat out,' he says.

What sort of boating could you do in these puddles?

'See that boat ramp?'

I glance at him. He's pointing up, not down. Way over there, quite high on the side of the valley with its craggy rim, I can see a length of concrete footpath that ends a good hundred metres above the sausage-shaped ponds. My jaw drops. We are sitting in the ute at the very bottom of the Cairn Curran Reservoir. This valley was once full of water. This is the reservoir whose construction brought Romulus Gaita, his wife, Christine, their small son, Raimond, and their friends the brothers Hora and Mitru all the way down here from Bonegilla migrant camp in 1950. And now it's empty. The water, like the grass, is gone.

I look about wildly. 'What's that small building, right up at the top?'

'That,' says Gaita with a tiny, inscrutable smile, 'was the Yacht Club.'

Gaita and his wife, Yael, have recently built a house on a bare rise only eight kilometres from Frogmore. This autumn evening as the sun goes down, sending long fingers of light across the stripped grey ground where a dozen tiny wrens are hopping and peeping in a bush, Gaita and I sit on the veranda, drinking wine. He spreads out on the table a sheaf of old black-and-white photos.

'Here's my father's *real* ironwork,' says Gaita, 'rather than the garden settings he made for a living in Australia.' It's a beaten iron sign hanging on the façade of a building in Europe: so intricate and deft that it looks like something in nature, the flourishing tip of a branch.

Like Kodi Smit-McPhee's face, the family photos are hard to look at without emotion: unbearably poignant, some touched with a gentle playfulness, others starkly dramatic.

'Here's my father when he was mad.' It's a tiny square headshot of a man from a Dostoevsky novel or a gulag: a dark face, thin, clenched, with blazing eyes and uptilted chin.

The striking picture of Romulus Gaita that was reproduced on the book's cover shows, in its original, a much more complex expression: a subtle play of humour and self-mockery around the mouth and eyes.

How handsome these people were! How *young*!

Christine Gaita is played in the movie by the German actress Franka Potente, who's blonde and strong faced. The real Christine, the photos seem to show, was tiny, almost delicate, with curly dark hair that puffed lightly on a breeze. In the book, Gaita describes her as 'highly intelligent, deeply sensuous, anarchic and unstable'. She plainly suffered from a mental illness: she heard voices, was self-destructively promiscuous, and aroused violent passions in men. In her son, whom she repeatedly left in the care of his father and Hora, she inspired an unassuageable longing: when she came back, and lay depressed in bed all day, unable to do the work of a wife and mother, he used to creep into the bed beside her, seeking the warmth of her body.

'I was always afraid Richard Roxburgh would romanticise my mother,' says Gaita. 'He was very struck by these photos. But I don't think he does.'

In fact Potente in the part is restrained almost to the point of self-effacement, as if the film did not quite dare to understand or fully to inhabit Christine. The scenes in which we see her inability to mother, though, made me close my eyes: the arms she dutifully holds out for her baby are two rigid prongs.

Yet at its heart the movie is an unflinching study of the suffering, the desperation and the decency of men. Its failings, which are several and very thought-provoking, are swept aside, for me, by its four splendid male performances—Eric Bana as Romulus, Russell Dykstra as Mitru, the sublime Smit-McPhee as Raimond, and Marton Czokas as Hora, Romulus's lifelong friend whose loving faithfulness radiates from both book and film.

'The builder who made this house,' says Gaita on the veranda, 'had read the book, and so had the young fellow who was labouring for him. One day towards the end of Hora's life I brought him up here to have a look at the building. I told the men he was coming. And when Hora got out of the car and walked towards the house, the builder downed tools and approached him like this'—Gaita bows his head and clasps his hands in front of him, like a man going up to take communion—'and the young labourer took his peaked cap off. I'd never before seen him without his cap.' He laughs, almost tenderly.

'How did Hora take it?' I ask.

'Oh,' he says, filling my glass, 'I don't think he noticed.'

On Sunday morning the magpies are shouting when we set out in the car on what I am beginning to realise is a highly structured visit to a series of personal shrines.

Gaita shows me the site of the long-gone camp where the Cairn Curran Reservoir labourers were accommodated, and the ramshackle hall opposite it, where dances were held and films shown. We visit his primary school, at which 'Professor Gaita' has recently instituted two awards: one for intellectual achievement, and the other the Romulus Gaita Prize for Kindness: 'though I did wonder,' he says, not quite joking, and I'm not quite sure if I should laugh, 'if it might be a *corrupting* prize—that kids might try to be kind for the wrong reasons.'

And then we head for Frogmore. He parks beside the bitumen road. We climb over a gate and walk a couple of hundred metres along a straight gravel track into the low, flat, empty landscape. My God, it's bleak out here. A steady, cool wind passes across the plain, coming from nowhere, going nowhere. Everything is brown or grey. Our boots crunch on the gravel. This is the road along which Christine Gaita trudged in her heels and waisted cotton dress, carrying her little suitcase, coming back to try again with her husband and son after each of her desperate flights to Melbourne.

'When I brought Nick Drake here,' says Gaita, 'it was a very hot day. The house had burnt down years ago. Scotch thistles had grown all over it. It was…desolate. It shocked me to see how desolate it was. I insisted on bringing him back another day, in softer light.'

'What sort of life did your mother expect or hope to have?' I ask.

'She'd been training as a chemist, in Germany.' His tone is carefully neutral. 'She thought she would have a city life. When I brought my aunt Maria here from Germany a few years ago, she didn't say much. She just cried. To think her sister had had to live in such a place.'

We climb through a wire fence. There's a small dam.

'Is this where you chucked your dad's precious razor?'

'This is the real dam,' he says, 'in which my father's real razor still lies rusting. Not long before he died he asked me again what happened to the razor. I just shrugged.'

'You *never told him*? You held out for forty years? What a power struggle!'

He looks surprised. 'I suppose it was.' He puts his head on one side, and gives his rare, endearing smile.

The burnt ruin of the house was demolished in 1969. The place where it stood is now just scraped-looking dirt strewn with old-fashioned brown beer bottles and studded with pieces of broken concrete, rusty iron and smashed crockery. A crumbly patina of sheep shit coats everything. We mooch about with our eyes on the ground. I long to pick up a piece of the china and put it in my pocket, but one does not steal souvenirs from shrines. A large lump is starting to form in my throat.

In the dirt near the fence lies the metal head of a spade, rusted away into a graceful curve like a palm tree. I pick it up by the shaft and hold it out to him.

'Look. How beautiful.'

'That,' he says in a noncommittal tone, 'is probably the one with which we buried Orloff.' In sentences of perfect syntax, as formally as if he were reciting a liturgy, he relates how the dog, which had taken a ground-glass bait, managed to drag himself as far as the outside of the wire fence, and died there.

'My father lifted him over the fence, so that he could be buried on the right side. It was the first time I saw my father cry. The only time we ever cried together was beside the grave of Orloff.'

Looking down at the unmarked ground where the bones of Orloff lie, I feel my self-control begin to slip. There's a loud squawk above our heads in the pine tree. We look up with a start. Two brilliant white cockatoos glide down from a high branch in a big showy curve. I glance at Gaita. Down his cheek is pouring a sheet of tears.

'I know it's silly,' he mutters, wiping them away with the back of his hand, 'but for a second I thought it was my cocky Jack. They can live for eighty or ninety years, you know.'

We stand there in silence, in the steady wind, heads down, hands in our pockets.

He drifts over to a huge pine that has toppled beside the dam. Its bare upper branches, trained sideways by decades of wind, look like thick grey hair streaming. Its roots are in the air, but its lower branches are still putting out cones and fresh green needles. The symbolism of this is so obvious that we can't even look at each other.

Once we have inspected the collapsing shed on the nearby farm, where Romulus Gaita laboured over a forge at his ironwork, and once we have peered through the smashed windows of the derelict house where Raimond was often invited to afternoon tea by the old ladies of the Lilley family, the morning is gone.

As we drive into Maryborough, I spot a white tower on a bushy hilltop.

'What's that?' I say, making conversation.

'That's the Pioneer Tower.' He keeps his eyes on the road. 'From which Mitru jumped to his death.'

We drive to its base. The observation deck at the top has been enclosed with white cyclone wire: Maryborough is a town whose economic base has collapsed, and whose young people know despair and have acted on it. We climb the stairs, stand awkwardly at the railing for a few moments, and hurry down again. We drive in silence down the old town's handsome streets, and then he steers the car on to the overgrown land along the railway line, behind a deserted flourmill.

'This,' says Gaita in his quiet, neutral voice, 'must be where they shot the bit with the pram'—a scene in which the boy Raimond, trundling a pram that contains his baby half-sister, hurries after his disturbed mother who has picked up a stranger in the street. She and the man disappear into a shed, and have sex against a wall. The frantic boy watches the encounter, with its violence and degradation, through a crack in the corrugated iron.

I don't know how much more of this I can take. I am struggling to hold on to some sort of self-command.

By the time we reach the cemetery and walk among the graves of these tragic people, Romulus, Hora, Mitru and, finally, near the fence, Christine, with its stone marked *She suffered deeply* (I read the dates, I do the sums; this woman killed herself a few weeks short of her thirtieth birthday), I am rigid with a distress so overwhelming that I know, with what's left of my mind, that it can't possibly be only mine. Some barrier between me and this man I hardly know has been breached by his story. I'm at the mercy of a tremendous force, a depth of sorrow that no book, no film can ever fully express or console.

Ritual behaviour is called for at shrines, but I can't think of a way to act. If we knew each other better, it would be natural for me to make some sort of human gesture of sympathy, or respect. But I'm paralysed by the fantasy of professional detachment, and by a strained sense of formality that I don't understand.

We stand side by side in front of Christine Gaita's grave.

Then Gaita moves slightly so that his shoulder lightly touches mine. I lean my shoulder against his. He puts his arm round my waist. I copy his movement, and we turn and walk back to the car like that, in silence, as if we were friends, though which of us is trying to comfort the other I have no idea.

2007

My Dear Lift-Rat

LAST week I had my hair cut. I was pleased, in the limited way one dares to be at this age. The next day my five-year-old granddaughter came home from kinder. She studied me up and down, and said with a crooked smile, 'I don't like your haircut, Nanna. You look like Luke Skywalker. It's dumb at the sides.'

The complex emotions provoked in a woman by this kind of remark have been recorded in literature by only one writer I know. Oh, there are sure to be others (Barbara Pym, for example, or Patrick Hamilton) who can strike a note of mortification and inject it with the tincture of the ridiculous that makes it bearable. But the one closest to my heart is Elizabeth Jolley.

It must have been the early 1980s when I first met Elizabeth. She was only four years younger than my mother. We lived on opposite sides of the continent, so we began to write to each other, and kept it up for twenty years.

She wrote flesh-and-blood letters, dipping an old fountain pen into a bottle of ink. She had an attractive hand, swift and slanting, with plenty of underlinings, and the same German-style capitals that she uses in her books on nouns she wants to stress—important words, like Birth, or School, or crashing Bore.

Once I told her, at an unhappy time, that I couldn't sleep. 'Don't just lie there,' she wrote back. 'Get up and make yourself a cup of Tea. Take a handful of Biscuits to the Desk and do your Tax Return.'

I've never said to her face how much her books mean to me, the spasms of mad laughter they provoke, the quiet tears of recognition and relief. I wrote about them in literary magazines, trying not to go over the top. She would write to thank me for the articles, in a formal way. Her manners are impeccable. I never knew whether she really liked them, or if she thought I had missed the point.

But I am still grateful for certain observations that she keeps returning to, throughout her work, leitmotifs that resound like quietly struck chords. To me they have the calming power of prayers.

'The strong feeling of love which goes from the parent to the child,' she writes in *My Father's Moon*, and again in that tiny, beautiful book *The Orchard Thieves*, 'does not seem part of the child which can be given back to the parent.'

'Water,' she says, 'is the last thing to get dark.' And my favourite: 'It is a privilege to prepare the place where someone else will sleep.'

Late in the 1990s, when I was living in Sydney, Elizabeth came to town for some literary event. We made a date to go out for dinner. I was to pick her up at her hotel, the swanky Hyde Park Hyatt where her publisher had installed her. I arrived in the lobby. No sign of a thin, tall, old lady in a loose cotton dress, with Roman sandals on her beautiful, bony feet. What was the polite thing? Should I go up to her room?

I approached the twin banks of lifts. The one at the far end landed with a discreet ping. Its door hissed open. Nobody appeared.

Then, in profile to me, a grey, bespectacled head poked out, like that of a rat cautiously preparing to leave its hole. It swung this way and that. Its eye caught mine. It was Elizabeth.

I won't try to describe what she would call our 'endless laughing fit', the way we staggered about the lobby on sagging legs. But from that evening on, she signed her letters 'Lift-Rat', and that's how I addressed her.

In 2000 and 2001 Elizabeth's letters grew fewer, and odder. She wrote indignantly about Hitler, how as a sixteen-year-old on holiday in Nazi Germany she had only escaped by 'being rushed to a small cargo ship'.

She told me that, 'like Ibsen and other writers', she had started having trouble 'remembering words and phrases'. Her spelling was shot. Her handwriting shrank to a scrawl.

'Destruction,' she wrote, 'can't go on forever.' Soon the letters stopped. Her son wrote to tell me that she had been diagnosed with dementia and admitted to a nursing home.

On a very hot February day in Perth, I was taken to Claremont to see her.

'You might get a shock,' they said. 'She won't know who you are.'

The only patient in a four-bed ward, she lay under a crisp white sheet with her head back on the pillow, her mouth open, her eyes closed. The veranda outside gave on to a shaded courtyard full of big old trees and strongly flowering shrubbery.

Pleasant airs came in through the open door. There was no airconditioning, and I was glad of this: she would hate to be shut away from the world of plants and grass that her work so quietly, so stoically praises.

I had never touched her, and I didn't touch her now. I stood at the end of the bed and looked at her. She was peaceful, cared for by people who loved and respected her. She didn't seem to be suffering; and she certainly didn't seem close to death.

But it was too late for me to say goodbye, or to thank her for the last sentence of *The Orchard Thieves*, where an old woman points out comfortingly to her daughter that the difference between a bad haircut and a good one is only a week.

2005

PART THREE

Dreams of Her Real Self

While Not Writing a Book
DIARY 1

The grandchildren I mention are Olive, Ted and Ambrose, aged at the time eight, four and two; they and their parents live in the house next door.

Early in the morning, after a heavy night of babysitting, I'm watering out the back when I hear a shuffling sound. Olive comes up behind me in her spotted dressing-gown and slippers, looking hunched and dramatic, and holding a sheet of paper in one hand. 'Read this,' she says. 'Dear Nanny I feel really Embarrased about last night and Ted got all the Books he wanted, all the games, and all the things he wanted and I didn't even get one single thing! And I would like you to acknowladge that. Lots of love Olive xxoo.'

I acknowledge it (it's true). She straightens her spine and runs off cheerfully. When I come inside I find her on the couch watching the end of *Close Encounters of the Third Kind*. Together we gaze at those bizarre sequences: the tiny 'scientists' in shirtsleeves and ties swarming everywhere on the landing site; François Truffaut in his neat, pale-tan bomber jacket; the communication by music, the mysterious riff played on a keyboard by the young nerd; the advance guard of smaller vessels; then the shimmering into view of the colossal spacecraft. I'm leaning forward, holding my breath, with a lump in my throat. The shining object opens its maw and the abducted earthlings stagger out: the navy men in their World War II uniforms who state name, rank and serial number—then the children—then *the dog*.

•

Jörg tells me that another translation of *sayonara*, the Japanese word for farewell, is 'if it must be'. He shows me a photo he has taken from a high hospital window during his chemotherapy: two blank buildings, and between them a band of clouded sky into which a big hot air balloon is rising, powered by a vigorous burst of flame. He makes no interpretation, of course, but I take it for an image of hope and self-propulsion.

•

Ted approaches me with a strange bashful smile and his eyes lowered. 'Nanny, you said to me that you always like my face.' 'I do. When I see it coming towards me I feel very happy.' He blushes, and can't stop smiling, or meet my eye. Soon we are aiming his cowboy pistols out the kitchen window at the red bucket on the woodpile, and firing with deadly accuracy. But when I say 'Peeeyow!' he corrects me: apparently only he is allowed to say 'Peeeyow'.

•

The cool change runs smoothly through the house. Outside, a shower of dried plum-tree petals swirls for a moment and falls.

•

On Radio National, constant talk of collapsing financial markets. Fran Kelly asks a politician what this will mean in pragmatic terms. 'Fran,' he says, 'you're going into the end of the world as we know it. I'm not going to follow you there.' I start thinking I should withdraw my cash from the bank, wrap it in thick plastic, and stash it in the roof space or bury it in the yard. My son-in-law says patiently, 'Everybody must want to do that. And that's exactly what they *don't* want you to do.'

·

In a fashionable café, five men in shirts and ties sit near me at a circular table. First I think they are having a business meeting. Then I realise they are praying.

·

I ride my bike to collect Ted from crèche. He emerges from the playground red-faced, in a lather of sweat. The teacher whispers that he has refused all day to take off his jacket because he didn't want to get dirt on the rodeo shirt with pearl studs and blue piping that I brought him from Newcastle. He has sweated so much, under his regulation Foreign Legion sunhat, that his eyebrows are flattened and misshapen. He is lost in a cowboy fantasy. As we fly home across Royal Park he says, in a voice forlorn with longing, 'Nanny. Do you know where they sell spurs?' Later, on the couch, I make up a story about an old lady who finds a cowboy baby lying forgotten by the roadside. She takes it home and raises it—gives him spurs, chaps, a lasso, some guns, which he fires only responsibly, and bullets that he always takes out and keeps in a drawer. When he's eighteen he gets a horse. He thanks the old lady, mounts the horse and clops away into the desert, looking for work rounding up cattle. She stands waving at the sliprail fence. He requests this story again and again, curled up in my lap with his thumb in his mouth.

·

Rod is visiting from Spain. We sit outside a café in Bourke Street for an hour. The angle of the afternoon light shows that his skin is forming tiny parallel wrinkles, very delicate and beautiful, and somehow poignant. He tells me that his four-year-old grandson is greatly exercised by the whereabouts of the police. The family traces this to the fact that one day his kindergarten teacher found her bag had been rifled by an intruder; she called the police and, when they arrived, the little boy thought they had come because he had done poo in his pants.

•

A conversation with the kids about the ubiquity of farts.

Me: 'I wonder if there's anywhere in the world where farting is polite.'

Olive: 'Maybe somewhere it could be a worship.'

•

In the expensive shoe shop, a woman of mature years is slumped sideways in a chair with her head on its armrest, sound asleep. Beside her a slightly younger woman, attended by a shop assistant, busily continues to try on shoes. Her unembarrassed physical proximity to the sleeper seems to indicate that they're companions, or even sisters. To let yourself go out like a light in a public place! How enviable! How free! I edge closer. Her upper lip, like mine, is an open fan of wrinkles. I would like to cover her gently with a cotton blanket.

•

In the morning it rains. Ambrose has passed his whole two years of life in drought. He looks up at the ceiling and says in a surprised voice, 'Noise!'

•

Jacob's funeral at Springvale. The building is very crowded. Two old women squeeze their way into the seats in front of ours. Another old lady murmurs to them, 'Excuse me, I'm saving these two places for my friends.' One of the interlopers, whose hair is dyed bright red, turns to her and snaps, 'Look, this is a funeral, not a party.' The service moves along with a brisk grandeur. Then we all file out, hundreds of us, and walk slowly along the cemetery roads to the open grave. Even at the back of the crowd we still flinch at the hollow thud when the first spadeful of earth strikes the coffin. I can't believe Jacob's body is really inside it. He had such bright eyes.

Later Ambrose wants to stay the night at my house. He won't go to sleep in the cot. I pick him up, wrap him in the blue rug, and hold him on my lap on the couch. Outside it's still light, but cloudy, as if about to storm. I sing him 'The Tennessee Waltz'. His eyes slide shut. His thumb slips out of his mouth and a few nerve tremors run through his left hand. He begins to breathe deeply, then to snore. Meanwhile, Jacob is out there at Springvale under all that dirt. A cool wind is blowing. I still think cremation is more bearable. The beloved one is only air, and some dry crumbs of inoffensive matter.

•

I watch *High Noon* again on DVD. Gary Cooper solemn, dogged, pained. The white, dusty streets he strides along, ever more hopeless. The scene where he writes his will.

•

At two in the morning, Ted, sleeping in the spare room, has a bad dream and creeps into my bed. He flings himself about diagonally for the rest of the night, cramming me into a tiny corner. God damn it, I think at 5 a.m., this is worse than being married.

•

Psychoanalyst at conference: 'Paradise has not only been lost, it never existed.'

•

Am I imagining an unusual quiet over the city? A breathlessness? The world is waiting for the news: will the US elect a black president? I hardly dare turn on the TV. But when I do I sit there and sob out loud. Tears absolutely pop out of my eyes. Olive comes in the back door and gazes at me curiously. 'I'm crying with happiness,' I say, 'because of Obama. Obama! OBAMA! To think I'm alive when this happened! It's better than men walking on the moon!' She puts down what she is carrying, approaches me with an ironical little smile, and gives me a mature hug, patting my shoulder. In this she is so like her mother that I cry even more.

•

One young woman to another, walking along Bridport Street: 'So I said to him, "If I wasn't your girlfriend, I'd be really concerned about your sexuality."'

•

I bring home some chocolates shaped like pyramids. Ted comes in to ask me for one. He struggles to articulate their shape, and comes up with 'a desert point'.

•

At David and Jason's in Newcastle, Jason makes me watch a few songs from Kylie's Homecoming Tour. It's a bloated spectacle of lights like a Nazi rally, the 'dancing' vulgar and clumsy, the songs a series of tiny ideas inflated beyond any possibility of meaning, and Kylie herself a minuscule creature with a very pretty profile and a surprisingly sweet smile. Now that she's had breast cancer and lost her French boyfriend, she looks almost interesting, her face thinner, darker, shadowed perhaps by adult pain and loss. I find her endearing. David is bored by her. But Jason adores her and seems proud of her. He shows Olive a single sequin that flew off her costume and into his hand when he was in the front row. Together they examine it, reverently, like a religious relic.

•

As the vodka kicks in I begin to make plans. I will go to my office and start work at eight every morning. I will stop drinking coffee and eating lollies. I will hire someone to pluck my eyebrows into shape once a week.

•

Library Week at the local primary school and I am invited to give a talk one afternoon. A boy of nine or so, in a dark-brimmed hat, sits in the front row. He is fidgety at first, then sits stiller and stiller, with his eyes fixed on my face. At the end he comes up with his parents, addresses me by my full name: they have a copy of my book that they would like me to inscribe.

Me: 'Is it *to* somebody?'

Boy: 'To our whole family, actually.'

Me: (pen poised) 'Will I write "To the whole family"?'

Parents: (shyly) 'Yes, that would be fine.'

Boy: (holds up one hand) 'NO.' (Looks from father to mother and back again, his eyebrows high. His voice goes up a few semitones.) 'No—we *agreed* that Helen Garner should write each name *individually*.'

Me: 'Okay, what are the names?'

Boy: 'Right.' (Takes deep breath.) 'The names are: Ross. Julie. They're my parents. Brady. Stuart. And Craig.'

Me: 'In that exact order?'

Boy: (firmly) 'In that exact order.'

Me: 'You're Craig, right? The youngest?'

Boy: (importantly) 'Yes, I am.'

I want to throw him across the back of my bike and speed away with him forever.

•

A thunderstorm at dawn! Roar of rain, drops dancing on the shed roof, the pear tree leaves springing and bouncing on their twiggy branches!

•

The family returns in the evening from three days at Wilsons Prom. Ted, exhausted from the long drive, dresses at once in cowboy gear, and comes through my back door in the dark with the rifle in one hand. 'Is anybody home? Where are you, Nanny?' He appears in the doorway of my workroom, very soft and peaceful. I sit him on my lap at the table. Long silences with the occasional remark. He has a *need* to dress as a cowboy. It calms something in him. I get out the photo album and we leaf through it, back and forth. He establishes a ritual response to every photo of his younger brother—a burst of unconvincing laughter.

•

Peter Porter on *The Book Show*: 'The purpose of form is to prevent you from putting down on the paper the first thing that comes into your head.'

•

My old Montblanc shorthand pen, the kind that's no longer made, disappears from my desk. It is my favourite fountain pen of all time. I search everywhere. Days later I have one last desolated look through the paper recycle bag beside my desk, and there it is. Calmly lying among the torn-up pages.

•

At the playground with Ted and the boys from round the corner. Francis, at three, has loose blond curls and a face of such louche, wry, heavy-lidded Irishness that I can hardly look at him without laughing.

I push him high on the swing. 'Higher. Higher,' he commands. In full flight he turns his head and calls to me over his shoulder in a seductive tone: 'Hey, Ted's nanny. Who's your best boy? Is it me?'

•

Barrie Kosky's production of Euripides' *The Trojan Women*. An ordeal of rape, blood, wailing and casual brutality. The moment that touches me most is when the little prince, in his suit and tie, is dragged into the cell where the Trojan women are imprisoned. Across the space he makes a tiny sign of recognition to his grandmother, the bruised and bloodstained queen, barelegged and barefooted in her fouled slip. The queen returns the gesture, the furtive showing of a flat palm. Soon after that, the child is hauled out to be thrown from the city walls.

•

Ted has been sick, some sort of gastric thing, and dozes all day on the couch. At dinner he sits at the table with the rest of us, but without plate or appetite, and begs for someone to play a game with him. Everyone refuses; they want to eat. He lays his little white cheek on the table and weeps. So his father gets him an old bank pay-in book and a pen, and he 'writes' out 'cheques' and 'plane tickets to America', silently concentrating, shoulders bowed, like a child clerk in Dickens, breaking all our hearts.

•

A tremendously famous and influential European critic lets my friend know that he admires his new novel. I'm thunderstruck. Imagine having the nerve to send the critic a copy! At whose feet would I lay my little tribute, if I dared? Janet Malcolm's? She scorched *The First Stone* in the *New Yorker* but I was so thrilled by the idea of her having read me that I felt no pain. God, how infantile. While I'm standing in the hall thinking about this, Ambrose with his pants off starts to thunder tempestuously on the piano. He yells for me to come. I enter the room. He leans forward, beaming over his shoulder, to display a large soft lump of shit he has just deposited on the piano seat.

.

At St Vincent's rapid response skin clinic I am to have a little lesion on my top lip investigated. A young Sri Lankan doctor without confidence but with a very sweet smile runs her cool fingers up and down my arms, and this way and that on my torso. The lesion has retreated and cannot be seen, no matter how hard she presses the magnifying glass on to my lip. A handsome male professor, very Australian, bursts into the cubicle. He spots the thing at once and diagnoses a solar keratosis. She still can't see it. He takes out his pen and draws a line round the keratosis, in ink that will not fade for hours. 'Get the gun,' he says. 'I'll come back in a minute and watch you do it.' The young woman stands beside me, timidly holding the liquid nitrogen cylinder in both hands. I do not want her to shoot my mouth with it, but before I can nerve myself to say so, the professor rushes back in. He seizes the gun from her, explains clearly and pleasantly how she should use it, then does the job himself in one well-aimed icy blast. Peeeyow.

.

In a Fitzroy pub on Sunday afternoon I become involved in a game of pinball with Ted. Two slightly bigger boys approach the machine. One looks at me narrowly, then says out of the corner of his mouth to his friend, 'That old lady thinks she can play. I'm going upstairs.'

.

A hot evening. I go to the gym on Racecourse Road for an 'assessment'. I don't belong in such a place. I feel a failure, someone labouring under a deluded idea of herself. In the harsh mirrors I look ugly and old, my hair cut too short, my lips held in an expression of contemptuous, defensive primness. I am put through my paces on the treadmill by one of those hulking young men with unblinking eyes who seem to become personal trainers. Then, as I begin to run and sweat, the irritating noises of the gym—horrible music, grunts of effort, shrill moronic laughter—fade into an oceanic roar. It dawns on me that this whole thing is about *going into a dream state*. My defences collapse.

∙

The unnerving silence of Christmas morning. No sound of traffic. Sun lies fresh on everything. Birds sing with unnatural sharpness. The air is still.

∙

At the health farm, fasting. I must be hallucinating: when I walk past a pile of folded towels I see them as a huge club sandwich. I present myself for a reiki treatment. The woman announces that she is going to massage my aura. I submit with a sigh. I don't have any trouble at all believing that people have auras: you only need to have seen a dying and then a dead body to know this. But I wanted the massage to be about my *gross earthly body*.

∙

Ted marches in my back door. 'I'm a cowboy. You can be my wife. I want something to eat. Will you cook this cattle meat I brought in?'

'Sure. How would you like it cooked, cowboy?'

'Toasted, please, with butter.'

∙

A picnic with a friend at the Botanic Gardens. Hot, clear day. We lie on rugs under a huge oak. I am wearing a faded pink linen shirt that I've always privately thought was rather becoming. She studies me in silence, and says, 'I'm sorry to tell you this, Hel, but that colour doesn't suit you. It makes your face look flushed. It makes you look older. This doesn't upset you, does it?' 'Well,' I say, 'I do feel a bit devastated.' She makes no response to this, and in a few moments our conversation turns to less fraught matters.

•

Ted on the swing: 'Come on! We need some attacking here! We need to explode some battleships!'

•

Two women of my age on the Craigieburn train are talking about how to make scones. I'm sitting right behind them, in an almost empty carriage. 'Your board's full of flour?' says the dark-haired one. 'And your hands are full of flour?' Her blonde friend, who has gold bangles on each wrist and very cared-for hands with big polished nails, expresses her utter helplessness in the face of *dough*. She reaches the point of confessing that she finds it repulsive to put her hands in it. They burst into a fit of laughter. The dark one keeps urging her friend not to give up. 'You don't have to handle it all *that* much.' She makes flat-palmed, downward gestures. The manicured one shudders extravagantly. As we pull into Southern Cross Station I get to my feet and stop beside them. 'Excuse me. I can't make scones either. First lot I made was perfect. Since then—disaster every time.' They welcome me into their paroxysms. The fair one touches my arm. 'Don't give up!' says the dark one. 'Try again!' From the platform, as I pass their window, I can see their teeth still flashing.

•

Ted: 'Nanny, Buzz told me that when people die they turn into gazombies.'

Me: 'Gazombies? That's not true. I'm quite old and a lot of people I know have died but not a single one of them turned into a gazombie.'

•

At a tram stop near Southern Cross a lovely Asian girl, perhaps still a teenager, with a fall of silky hair right down her back, is standing among the waiting passengers. A man in a T-shirt and jeans approaches her and tries with a dull, unsmiling belligerence to engage her in conversation. His questions strike a discordant note: 'Where are you going? How old are you?' I can't hear her replies, or even if she's making any. Two young women in business suits and heels, who have been chatting and laughing at the stop, step forward to the platform's edge and without breaking their flow of talk simply interpose their bodies between the importunate bloke and the girl. He moves off, sullen and confused. The women don't address the girl. In fact I'm not even sure that they noticed her predicament, but I choose to believe that they performed a spontaneous act of sisterly protectiveness.

.

Jörg and his wife, Keiko, sit with me in Marios. His skull is softly furred, his face purified, refined. The chemo appears to have worked. Nobody mentions elation, but the table our elbows are on is hovering a few inches above the floor.

.

Joan Acocella on the dancer Mikhail Baryshnikov: 'If there is a point in classical art where aesthetics meets morals—where beauty, by appearing plain and natural, gives us hope that we, too, can be beautiful…'

I resolve to spend the rest of my life searching for that point.

2011

Red Dog: A Mutiny

IN January my family next door went down the coast and left me in charge of our vegetable garden and their dog. Excellent. I would spend the summer reading novels on my bed, and every morning and evening I would take the red heeler to the park and make him run his furry arse off.

When Dozer first arrived from a rescue shelter in the Mallee, he flinched at sudden hand movements, and cowered if you came round the corner carrying the hose; but under a benevolent regime he soon became confident and calm. He was very, very good-looking, with large pointed ears, Amy Winehouse eye makeup, and leaf-shaped patterns of dark brown along his spine.

My son-in-law had once been the master of a legendary blue heeler called Tess, whose death in old age had prostrated him with grief for a fortnight. He and my daughter worked hard to train the red pup right. He would sit, lie down, stop, stay. He was an outside dog. The family drove away. I moved his gear from their back veranda to mine.

The summer was hot. At the park each morning, as the sun rose, he stepped out of the car and on to the grass with an unhysterical tread, and raised his face handsomely to the dry air. I hurled the ball into the blue, and away he flew.

He was so smart: he knew to stay off the bike path when the helmeted warriors came streaming through from the north, scattering curses. He was so obedient: a faint whistle between my teeth and he was at my side. He was so sociable, so sweet natured: one day a svelte young whippet took a shine to him; flowing alongside him as they raced, she got a grip on the loose skin of his cheek and hung on. I quailed against a tree trunk, but he remained nonchalant, grinning down at the weightless parasite. They sped in tandem to the far end and returned at a canter, all smiles.

He was a heavy-chested, square-set dog. Neither of us liked a leash. Of course I always had one on my person. But it was only a token. The dog and I understood each other. He was at my back door at six every morning, not whining or barking, just breathing with his mouth open. He knew not to barge between the car's front seats as I drove. With the Chuckit I bought at the pet shop my throws became magnificent. While he tore about after the ball, I stood in the park's centre, cracking jokes with a loose group of humans. Perhaps they even accepted me. The breeze skimmed across the mown grass and rustled the coloured plastic shit-bags we had tied to the curved handles of our launchers.

One morning, after a night of rain, it struck me that our routine had become rigid. Was there nothing in a dog's life but work? I left the ball and the launcher in the laundry. I clipped the leash round my waist and we set out for the park on foot.

At first he kept looking back over his shoulder, waiting for me to produce the ball. When I made it clear I hadn't brought it he accepted my ruling, and trotted down the sloping streets in the dark, running and swerving at random, sniffing posts and pissing on them, following trails the way dogs are supposed to. We skirted the park and, as it started to get light, headed up the steep lane towards home. Behind the high school I saw the first cars zip through the roundabout. I unwound the leash from my overalls and called him. He propped. He gave me a stare I couldn't read. And when I grabbed his collar and clipped the leash on to the ring, he burst into a rage.

He got the leash between his jaws and dragged, dragged at it, growling and panting. He hauled it behind me, whirled it this way and that so I was spun around. He yanked it, threw his weight back on his haunches so the woven fabric stretched tight between us. I shouted his name. His teeth were bared to the ears, his brow lowered over the savage shine of his black eyes.

Astonished, I fought him for the leash. Close to me in our twisting struggle he bit me, twice on the left forearm, twice on the right, bang, bang, not skin-breaking bites but blunt blows, like punches. I cried out. I held my ground beside him, gripping the leash, and rapped out the only command left to me: 'Sit! Sit!'

He sat. It held, the fragile structure of his training, though his eyes burned fiercely up at me from the level of my thigh. My heart was going like mad. I let him off the leash. He scampered across the road and I followed like a supplicant.

We had another two blocks to go. He ran ahead of me, co-operating at corners. Once he grabbed the dangling sleeve of my raincoat and gave it a sharp wrench. Several times he dawdled till I caught up, then threw himself heavily against my legs, jostling me with the full weight of an angry cattle dog. We crossed the railway bridge and he gave up on me, ran on ahead in scorn, tail high, head in noble position. I limped behind, shaking and sweating, still holding the leash.

Early next morning, with embarrassing bruises on each arm that would keep my sleeves rolled down for a week, I returned to the exact custom that I had first established and then flouted. Since that day, at home and out in the world, he has behaved towards me with impeccable grace and affection. But we both know that the compact between us has been broken. He senses that, beneath my crisp commands, I have lost my nerve. He likes me. He needs me. He humours me. But I am afraid that somewhere in his wild dog's heart, he secretly despises me.

2012

Funk Paradise
DIARY 2

The kids are now twelve, eight and six.

On Friday night I have a ticket to a Melbourne Symphony Orchestra concert. On my way out the door I say to my son-in-law, 'I'm going to hear *The Rite of Spring*.' Pulling on his Western Bulldogs beanie he retorts, 'I'm going down to Docklands to see *The Rite of Winter*.'

•

At the bakery Anita serves me. She hasn't been at work for a while. I ask if she has been ill. She glances left and right. I am the only customer. She says in a low voice, 'I've been at home for two weeks. I had breast reduction surgery.' I withstand the urge to drop my eyes to her chest. 'Wow! Are you pleased?' She lowers her great heavy lids, and across her goddess's face, beautiful in a tremendous, mythological way, passes a wave of relief and pleasure. 'Helen, I couldn't go on any more—my *shoulders*.' I gaze at her in wonder. 'I look,' she says, 'like I did when I was sixteen!' I permit myself to glance down. Two lovely firm round globes ride at a youthful level under her pastel uniform. 'You look gorgeous,' I say with a sigh. Kirsty, meanwhile, is busy further along the counter, eyes on her work, smiling with secret benevolence.

•

At lunchtime I go over the road to the hospital cafeteria for a sandwich, and get talking to an Indian volunteer called Harjinder. He looks about fifty, with wavy grey hair, very warm-faced and appealing. He's a small-scale builder by trade, self-employed, and volunteers one day a week. He hopes that when he's known and trusted he will get into 'more interesting parts of the hospital, like Emergency'. He tells me he gets on well with 'women of all ages' because, when he and his Australian wife first got together, she said, 'The only way to have a happy marriage is for you to have women friends. Talk with them, listen to them. That's how you'll learn what women are like, and what they need.'

•

I pedal over to Kensington just after dark. As I roll along the lane towards the railway underpass, a young Asian woman on her way home from the station walks out of the tunnel towards me. After she passes there's a stillness, a moment of silent freshness that feels like spring.

•

Conversation with grandson. 'You've got beautiful hair, Teddy. It's really *beautiful*.' 'I know dat.' 'How do you know?' Long pause. 'I look in de mirror.'

•

Reading Shostakovich, the savage distortions of the way he had to live and work under Stalin. A formidable voice—a voice one would dread to hear. It provokes shudders of fear, a sort of revulsion. But one reads on, ashamed to put it down. 'I don't want to deny that I went through a bad period. Perhaps the careful reader will understand that, or perhaps he'll just skip all this rubbish and think, munching a chocolate, "Whatever made me read this book? It's just upsetting me before bedtime."' At times he is weirdly funny. 'Composing by tape recorder is a special taste, like licking rubber boots.' A joke about a king who, hearing that a famously tedious person is travelling to see him, abdicates.

•

My niece brings me her baby to mind for two hours. All serene until the final thirty minutes, when she gets thirsty. Because she is totally breastfed, nothing I offer is acceptable. Only her mother will do. She screams for twenty minutes without stopping. Her little dark head keeps swivelling on its neck, searching, searching. If I carry her into a different room she swings her gaze around it and bursts into fresh cries of despair.

•

A dark sky, striped low down with bands of translucent pearly grey and the faintest, driest yellow. Bare plane tree branches disposed against it, as in a painting.

•

On the couch I watch ep after ep of *Mad Men*. Don Draper goes to California and falls in with some Eurotrash layabouts who on the DVD case are described as 'exciting new friends' but are in fact shallow bores. Roger dumps his wife and goes off with a secretary who is vain about her looks and fancies herself as a poet: languorous sensuality and all the rest. I lie here, a batty old nanna, shouting at the screen: 'Do NOT get into that car.' 'Oh, shut up, you stupid idiot.'

But when it's over I set up the board and, in the spirit of Betty Draper, iron the pillowcases.

.

At a conference I meet a Supreme Court Judge who tells me he lives in what is now known in real estate advertisements as 'the *Monkey Grip* house', where many important events of my life took place. He is renovating it. I ask him about the rooms. He lists them: 'And there's a room behind the big front one, that's too small to be used for anything but a bathroom. My daughter used to have her desk in there.'

Me: 'You mean the one with the wooden shutter on the window?'

Judge: 'Yes.'

Me: (in the low, falsely humble tone of the former hippie) 'That used to be my bedroom.'

.

After the summer of the terrible bushfires, the kids at the crèche became deeply interested in death. They got into their heads the belief that if a dead body burned, it would go on burning forever.

.

Respected Radio National reporter: 'I see myself as a worker bee at the coalface of journalism.'

.

Tom and his brother Phil get mugged in Lygon Street, around midnight, by a man in a balaclava. Tom hands over his money and his phone, and turns to run away. That's when the robber stabs him. Sticks a knife into his back, just below his left shoulderblade. Later, the robber makes calls to the girls whose numbers are in the phone.

.

My friend's ten-year-old son reports, with severe disapproval, that a boy in his grade has suddenly 'got a girlfriend'.

Father: 'Oh, it's probably pretty nice for him, though, isn't it?'

Son: 'But Dad, everyone knows that grade-four relationships have got very little going for them, in terms of meaning.'

•

In the café with Tony, I notice at a nearby table a young woman, barely out of her teens, and her remarkably plain boyfriend (in a suit). She has a perfect oval face, hazel eyes, and one of those exquisite European mouths that in my youth did not exist on Australian women: soft, fleshy, petal-like, almost circular. I admire her, dreamily. Then she leans forward to her boyfriend and says in a vain, nasal, flirtatious voice, 'Do you think about me when you're at work?' Tony blanches and mutters, 'Run, mate! Run now! Run a thousand miles!'

•

Someone has published a biography of Muriel Spark. God, what a miserable piece of work she sounds, and yet whenever the reviewer quotes a line of her writing, the room lights up. Apparently her letters make no reference whatsoever to current events. So?

•

My sister stays with me while she's on jury duty in a three-day trial. I am mad with envy: I've never even been called. She is made foreperson: 'You're a musician,' they say to her. 'You're used to standing up in front of strangers.' She cries on the train home, tired and anxious. 'There's so much riding on it, but they don't give us enough information.' She is honourable and won't tell me about the case, but speaks with astonishment of the laziness and stupidity of one of the jurors. Before they start to deliberate, the woman says, 'Let's make a pact. Let's make a fast decision, so we can get out of here.' The others look at her in silent contempt.

•

'Did you lose your bracelet round here?' This printed sign, sticky-taped to a lamppost near the station, gives me the same citizenly pleasure that I get from reading, in the information section of my Filofax, 'Glove sizes are the same in every country.'

•

At a local arts festival a man wants to stage an event called The Writers' Pyre. Writers would line up at a large bonfire to burn a document—a diary, a letter, or perhaps a failed draft—having first read it out loud and explained why they were burning it. I am thrilled by this proposal. Will they invite me to take part?

•

On the train to the city on Saturday night, a bunch of girls dressed in fantastical costumes are running about and shrieking. It must be a hens' night. A bedraggled street person sitting near us reports that they have been shouting out men's names—'Anyone called Steve?'—and blokes of that name get up and have their photo taken with the girls. They must have risked an Ali or a Muhammad: a young Muslim man stands up for the camera. He is tall and handsome and rather shy. When a screaming girl in a bridal veil seizes him round the neck and presses her cheek to his, he submits with good humour, but his arm dangles limply between their torsos. At the next stop he gets off and walks past our window smiling faintly to himself, like a man after an ordeal that he feels he has negotiated successfully.

•

The kids and I watch a DVD of black-and-white Felix the Cat cartoons from the '20s. Their brilliance is primitive, hilarious—an army of sausages that marches, relentless and interminable, against the citadel of the rats. I am struck by the repeated theme of a male cat falling in love with a seductive female, then discovering that she already has scores of teeming offspring. One disillusioned suitor commits suicide by lying down outside a power station and plugging a gas pipe into his mouth. Another leaps into the arms of a butcher and says, in a crudely lettered speech balloon, 'I had a lucky escape!' Weird male anxiety in these tales. I look for the artist's name. Pat Sullivan. An Irish Catholic?

•

Five shaven-headed Buddhist nuns in glasses and curry-coloured robes sit in a row at the airport, rubbing skin cream into their hands. Each nun has her own tube.

•

Martin in the Cellar Bar tells me that the cardiologist had to stop his heart—turn it off, turn it back on. At his bedside, before the procedure, the doctor said, 'People say this is the most horrible experience of their lives. A sense of approaching doom. Just so you know. But I've done this many times. I'm very experienced—' At that instant his arm bumped the cannula in Martin's hand, and a spout of blood gushed out of it, soaking the front of the doctor's gown. We both crack up. Martin's medical experiences are beyond appalling—yet there he sits in his heavy spectacles, grinning at me with all his teeth. I've been laughing with him in the Cellar Bar for thirty years. There's no reason why we should ever stop.

•

Sally gives me a new Tom Jones CD which to my astonishment contains two songs of such funky splendour and huge horn sections that I dance wildly by myself in the kitchen. I wish there could be a club in a plain-looking suburb where you would walk through the door on a Friday night and find a funk paradise—everyone you've ever liked or loved or slept with or rejected or been rejected by, adorable people you've never met, strangers looking into each other's faces and bursting out laughing, detectives and journos in suits struttin' with their elbows out, gangs of Asian students, dignified old Jewish couples, backpackers from every land, lonely boys and bored teenage girls rushing out on to the floor. All crippling thoughts of cool would explode and vanish, and everything would be forgiven, everything redeemed.

2012

Dreams of Her Real Self

IT was always clear to me what would happen when my parents died.

Dad would pitch forward without warning into the grave he had dug with his knife and fork. The struggle that had shaped and distorted my character would be over. I would be elated to see the back of him. Then I would torture myself with guilt for the rest of my life.

Free of his domineering presence, my mother would creep out from under her stone. She would show herself at last. At last I would know her. Shyly she would befriend her five remaining children, maybe even come to live with one of us. She would take up her golf clubs again, pull on her flowery bathing cap and swim in the surf, simmer her modest vegetable soups, knit cardigans in quiet stripes with a lot of grey. In a few years she would fade, weaken and slip away. Surely, about her, I would feel only a mild sorrow that would pass in the manner that nature intended.

•

She went first.

She was in her early eighties when Dad dragged her to the last of the scores of dwellings he had imposed on her during their long marriage: a seventh-floor apartment in central Melbourne that in a fit of Schadenfreude he had bought from a member of her family whose finances had hit the wall. Isolated up there, with a view of St Patrick's cathedral and Parliament House, she sank into a stunned, resentful gloom shot through with bitter sarcasm. She would point at a gin and tonic on the table and say, in a grim, warning tone, 'Mark my words. In a minute that ice is going to melt. Then the glass will overflow, and there'll be a *hell* of a mess to clean up.' She slumped into depression, then drifted away into dementia. She wandered at night. She fell and fractured a bone. Her body withered. In a nursing home she became savage, bestial. She snarled at us and lashed out with her claws. Lost to herself and to us, she died at last, by means of something I can only call chemical mercy. My youngest sister and I, strained and silent, chanced to be the only ones at her bedside when she exhaled her last hoarse breath.

.

People we had hardly seen since childhood, friends she had left behind in obedience to Dad's driven restlessness, came to her funeral. They spoke of her with tender faces.

.

After she died, we persuaded our father to sell his flat and buy the shabby little house next door to me. He was too proud to be looked after and he didn't like my cooking. But for two years he flourished. He zoomed to the neighbourhood cafés on a motorised scooter. He came to hear a blues band at the Elwood RSL. He began to keep company with a woman he had fancied before he married Mum, a stylish widow from Geelong who was not afraid to take it right up to him. He had to ask his daughters for advice on his love-life. He liked a spontaneous drive to the country to look at the crops. In the car we were always laughing.

One scorching summer morning, at breakfast time, he told me he hadn't been able to get his breath in the shower. I called an ambulance and knelt down to strap his sandals on him so he could walk out of there like the man who owned the joint, but they put him on a gurney, and the only person who dared refer to the thunderingly obvious fact that he was never coming back was one of the paramedics, who said to my granddaughter, as we stood hand in hand on the footpath watching them load him into the ambulance: 'Want to kiss Great-Grandpa goodbye?'

On Hoddle Street his heart stopped. The paramedics got it going and swept into St Vincent's Emergency. The family rushed in. He was ninety-one: the doctors decided to take him off the ventilator. We stood around him in a tearful circle. They whisked out the tube. He took a huge shuddering gasp, and began to breathe strongly. The doctors and nurses joined in our shout of laughter. The stubborn old bull would never die. He was admitted to a room on the seventh floor. That evening the others went down to the street for a meal and I stayed with him. He was unconscious, breathing without help in a steady rhythm. A nurse came in to check on him. While she bent over him to smooth the sheet under his chin, I moved away from the bed and went to look out the window of the high, west-facing room. The sun was going down in a blaze over the Exhibition Gardens. He breathed in. He breathed out. He was silent. I turned and said, 'He's gone.' The nurse, surprised, felt for his pulse. 'Yes. He's gone.' She left the room. I blessed him. I sat with him quietly for ten minutes, on a chair near the window. Then I started texting the others to come back.

•

My father's mother died, in Hopetoun, when he was two. He had a sternly loving stepmother, but there was always something of the abandoned child about him. He was as entitled and as quick to anger as a toddler. He was jealous, impatient, rivalrous, scornful, suspicious. He could not trust anyone. He could not keep friends; by the end of his life, he had none. He was middle class, a wool merchant, with money but no education. He never read a book. One of my husbands, put through Dad's insulting third degree about whether he was 'living off' me, said he was a peasant. Yet with strangers he had great charm: 'I thank you, sir, from the bottom of my heart.' He had an unerring ear for music, though he never sang, except ironically. He was a good ballroom dancer. He could shape a story. He liked to laugh: 'I've never *seen* such a deflated manager.' On Mum's headstone it seemed right to mention the word *love*. For his, we could not find a short phrase to encapsulate his contradictions, our exhausting struggles. We ended up with *Our father, a boy from the Mallee*. People who had not known him were startled by the bluntness of the epitaph. But to me, at least, it evokes a landscape of complex meaning, forlorn, sometimes beautiful: a desert that now and then bloomed.

·

I set out to write about my mother, but already I am talking about my father.

He is easy to write about. He was a vivid, obstreperous character whose jolting behaviour was a spectacle, an endurance test that united his children in opposition to him. Things he did or failed to do gave rise to hundreds of stories that we still share and embellish.

To write about her at length, coherently, is almost beyond me. He blocked my view of her, as he blocked her horizon. I can think about her only at oblique angles and in brief bursts, in no particular order.

·

When my daughter was a teenager she had a dog, a poodle cross called Polly. Polly fell down the crack between two of my marriages. She trudged again and again across inner Melbourne to my ex-husband's house, and died a lonely, painful death, by misadventure, in a suburban backyard. She was an anxious creature, timid and appeasing, who provoked in me an overwhelming impatience. She would lie at my feet, tilting her head on this angle and that, striving for eye contact. The more she begged for it, the less I could give.

In just such a way, over many years, I refused my mother eye contact. She longed for it. I withheld it. I lacerate myself with this memory; with the connection I can't expunge between lost mother and lost dog.

•

When, in the street, I see a mother walking with her grown-up daughter, I can hardly bear to witness the mother's pride, the softening of her face, her incredulous joy at being granted her daughter's company; and the iron discipline she imposes on herself, to muffle and conceal this joy.

•

Time and again Elizabeth Jolley has observed that 'the strong feeling of love which goes from the parent to the child does not seem part of the child which can be given back to the parent'. But last spring, at a big and brilliant community show to celebrate the reopening of Melbourne's concert hall, a clever conductor divided the audience and taught us to sing in parts. A thousand euphoric strangers sang, in time and in tune, a slowly modulating melody. In the row in front of me sat an old woman and her daughter. Too absorbed in singing even to glance at each other, they reached, they gripped hands, they did not let go until the song was done.

•

A few years before she entered her final decline, my mother and I went together to hear a famous string trio. We arrived early, took our front-row seats high in the gallery, and looked down at the stage. It was bare, except for three chairs. My mother said, 'Looks a bit sad, doesn't it.' Surprised, as if at a witticism, I swung to face her. She raised her eyebrows and grinned at me. We both began to laugh. I was filled with respect. Whenever I remember that moment, the hopeless thing in my heart stops falling, and finds a small place to stand.

•

I came home from university armed with the baroque. Bach and Vivaldi, their stringent impersonality, made my mother's favourite records sound overemotional and corny. Now, if I turn on the car radio and hear Tchaikovsky or Brahms, I find tears running down my cheeks. Perhaps that's where I can find her, take her hand and walk with her: across the fields and through the splendid forests of the Romantic piano concertos she loved.

•

She was not confident, or quick. She did not sense the right moment to speak. She did not know how to gain and hold attention. When she told a story, she felt a need to establish enormous quantities of irrelevant background information. She took so long to get to the point that her listeners would tune out and start talking about something else. Family shorthand for this, behind her back, was 'and then I breathed'.

•

Shows of affection were not done in our family. We could not even hug without an ironic shoulder pat. Expressions of emotion were frowned upon. 'You great cake. Pick up your lip before you trip over it.' I saw her, as an old woman, have to muster the courage to hold out her arms for someone else's baby. Perhaps this is why she never knew that her grandchildren loved her. She was shy with them. Once she said to me, in her patient, timid way, 'I don't think they like me much.'

Only last week, though, there floated into my awareness, from a cache of treasures Dad had left behind, a little tribute that their youngest granddaughter, my nine-year-old niece, had written in the week before Mum died. It is accompanied by a drawing: a roast chicken on a rug, and far in the background two figures, one large and one small, walking away hand in hand. 'Me, Grandpa and her went on picnics in the sun, just near her house in Kew. The sun was bright and the food was delicious, mostly chicken and potatoes and sometimes delicious sandwiches. Then we would go back home and read or watch telly. But what I liked was often we would go into her room and look in the cupboards and see all theese speicial things of hers some belonging to her six children one of which is my mum. I love all six of them and give them my best dreams of Grandma, dreams of her real self, the self with no evil diaseases, the strongest part of her body and everyone should know its still here.'

•

Probably she was afraid of me. I went to university, the first of her children to move beyond her ability to contain, or help. In 1972 I was fired from the Education Department for answering my students' questions about sex. There were cartoons for and against me in the newspapers. She showed me a letter of protest she had laboriously written to the editor of the *Age*. The letter revealed that she had not understood the irony of the cartoons. The one she most hated was the one that most strongly defended me. I tried to explain this gently, but I knew she was humiliated. To be her intellectual superior was unbearable.

•

I was the eldest of six children. They kept coming. I must have been taught to change a nappy, fill a bottle, wheel a pram, rock an infant to sleep. I cannot remember there ever being a baby in the house.

·

The clean, simple architecture of Victorian baby health centres has always comforted me.

·

When my daughter was born, I was estranged from my father, who had tried to prevent me from marrying my first husband, thus mortally offending his decent and generous parents. My mother had defied him and come to our wedding, at which one bottle of champagne sufficed for the entire company; but at the time of our baby's birth she was unable to break through his veto. She did not come to the hospital. I don't remember hoping that she would, or being upset that she didn't. Years later my youngest sister told me she recalled, as a very small girl, sitting in the car outside my house with our father, waiting for Mum to come out. So she must have fought her way past him. I have no memory of her visit.

·

Towards the end of Mum's life, when she was becoming vague and fearful but was not yet demented, my widowed sister Marie was often harsh with her in a way that made me flinch: the grief of her widowhood had stirred up some old rage in her that I did not understand. One day Mum asked Marie to drive her down to the Mornington Peninsula, to visit our aunt. She obliged. Next time I saw Mum, she told me, without complaint and in a puzzled tone, that when Marie had delivered her home after that outing, she had brusquely put her hand out for petrol money.

Last year I went to the Australian War Memorial in Canberra. I had expected dusty old weapons and dioramas of heroism. Instead

I found a curatorial work of inspired brilliance and grandeur, and a chapter of my mother's life that I had never before bothered to fit into the history of the twentieth century. At the desk I told the attendant the name of my uncle Noel, Mum's favourite younger brother, who was killed in World War II. Our parents rarely spoke of him. Dad was in a reserved occupation; was the war a touchy subject? But when he was very old, he told me that Mum had been devastated by her brother's death. She never got over it; he was 'like her twin'.

The man at the war museum turned to a computer, pressed a few keys, and handed me two sheets of paper. Flight-Sergeant. Aerial Gunner RAAF. Cause of death: Flying Battle. Lancaster crashed at Hollenstein, Germany, while returning from a raid over Brunswick on 12/13 August 1944, killing all crew members. At last I registered the dates. I had to sit down. He must have been barely twenty. When my mother got the news that his plane had crashed, I would have been a toddler of eighteen months, and my sister an infant, five weeks old. How could she have mothered us, staggering under such a blow? In her old age Mum said to me, 'Marie was a very thin and *hungry* baby—always crying and wanting more.'

•

Once, while my mother was staying a weekend with me, a man I was having an affair with came to see me. He behaved sweetly towards her, questioned her about her life. He asked about her childhood and her family. How had the news of her brother's death in the war come to her: by phone, or was there a letter? She seemed astonished that someone should be interested in her. When he left, she turned to me and said, '*He's* nice.' 'He's the love of my life, Mum,' I burst out, 'but he's married.' I suppose I thought she would disapprove. But she cried, 'Oh!' She leapt off her chair and threw her arms around me. She said, 'Just wait.'

From what life experience, from what instinct she drew this spontaneous advice I have no idea.

She got on well with all the men in my life, and they liked her. She continued to have warm feelings for them, and they for her, years after they and I had wrecked everything and gone our separate ways.

•

For my work, on tram stops, in planes, I'm not afraid to question any stranger. But I never sat my mother down and pressed her about the past, her life before me, before our father.

•

One evening she and Dad and I came out of a restaurant. The street was empty of traffic for a mile in each direction. I stepped confidently off the kerb but she seized the tail of my jacket and pulled me back. 'We'll cross at the lights. I'm a very. Law-abiding. Person.'

•

My mother was good at sewing. When I was five or so she made me a pair of pyjamas on her Singer machine. I refused to wear them because they had frills on the bottom. She pleaded with me. She told me that if I wore the pyjamas, fairies would come and they would like me because of the frills. I did not care about the fairies. Even at that age I sensed the guilty power my refusal gave me.

•

It seemed to me, as a child, that our mother was hopeless at giving birthday parties. The cakes she made weren't right. The decorations and games somehow missed the mark. Other kids' mothers knew how to do a party right but Mum didn't. Instead of her plain cupcakes with icing, I secretly thought, she should have made those cakes with whipped cream and little tilted wings on top that other girls' mothers presented. It was a very strong sense I had, that there was something she did not get. All my adult life I despised myself for my disloyalty. It did not comfort me to learn that all children felt their mothers to be socially lacking in some crucial way. But one day when she was old and we were talking about motherhood, she said with a casual little laugh, 'I was never any good at giving kids' parties. I somehow never had the knack.'

·

She used to wear hats that pained me. Shy little round beige felt hats with narrow brims. Perhaps one was green. And she stood with her feet close together, in sensible shoes.

·

Oh, if only she would walk in here now.

·

She must have been only in her late thirties when she developed a gum disease and had to have all her teeth extracted. If she had gone to a Melbourne dentist, instead of remaining loyal to the doddery old fellow who treated our family in Geelong, a less drastic treatment might have been found. Not only did he pull out all her teeth, he whacked the false ones in over her bleeding gums. She came home and sat by the fire, hunched in her dressing-gown, eyes down, holding a hanky to her mouth. We did not know how to comfort her. We tiptoed around her, whispering, going about our business. Thirty years later, at home on my own one night, I saw on SBS a movie called *Germany, Pale Mother* in which a woman in wartime had all her teeth removed as a cure for her neurasthenia. I sat breathless on the couch while the dentist in his white coat yanked out her teeth and dropped them one by one with a clang into a metal dish.

·

My sax-playing sister, a professional, came over last winter with her ukulele and a Johnny Cash CD. She sings in the eighty-voice Melbourne Mass Gospel Choir, but is highly sceptical of all things religious. She wanted me to listen to 'Wayfaring Stranger'. All I knew was that it is an old folk song of weariness, of sin; of the longing to cross over Jordan.

'Come on,' she said. 'It's only got a couple of chords. We can learn it in five minutes.'

I got my uke down off the shelf. We tuned up. Yes, it was easy, the music part.

'Listen to that harmonium-playing,' she said. 'It's exemplary.'

But the lyrics.

> *I know dark clouds will gather round me,*
> *I know my way is hard and steep.*
> *But beauteous fields arise before me,*
> *Where God's redeemed their vigils keep.*
> *I'm going there to see my mother.*
> *She said she'd meet me when I come.*
> *I'm just going over Jordan.*
> *I'm just going over home.*

I said nothing, just worked at getting the strum right. That night, after she'd left, I played along with Johnny Cash for a long time. I could hardly get the words out, but his voice, weary and cracked, gave the song a majesty that still welcomed the humble chords of a ukulele.

•

My mother was a natural athlete, neat, small and graceful. I was hopeless at sport of any kind. All I wanted to do was read and write. At fourteen I got my first typewriter, my grandmother's reconditioned Smith Corona portable. Mum asked me to type out the results of the Point Lonsdale Golf Club ladies' tournament, to be reported in the *Geelong Advertiser*. Perhaps she was trying to interest me in what she cared about, or was simply looking for something we could do together. At the time I took it at face value: my first typing job. We toiled together at the kitchen table after tea. She dictated, and I clattered away at my beautiful oil-scented machine, on the quarto paper of which we had bought a ream at Griffiths Bookstore. She did not lose her temper at my mistakes. I felt important and useful. We were pleased with each other when the job was done. Two mornings later we stood shoulder to shoulder, looking down proudly at the newspaper's inky columns.

·

I must have been about twelve when the insight came to me that my mother's entire life was divided into compartments. None of them was any longer than the number of hours between one meal and the next. She was on a short leash. I don't recall thinking that this would be my fate, or resolving to avoid it. All I remember is the picture of her life, and the speechless desolation that filled me.

·

Mrs Thatcher has told one of her interviewers that she had nothing to say to her mother after she reached the age of fifteen. Such a sad, blunt confession it seems, and yet not a few of us could make it. The world moves on so fast, and we lose all chance of being the women our mothers were; we lose all understanding of what shaped them.
     Hilary Mantel

·

The quietly mighty Japanese film director Yasujiro Ozu tells story after story of adult children breaking away from their parents. His characters rarely cry, or raise their voices. Their emotions are expressed in tiny signs and changes of position. A father looks down at his glass. A mother folds her hands, or draws a handkerchief from her sleeve. These subtle movements call up in me surges of excruciating sympathy for my parents, for the hurt, helpless, angry love they must have felt as they watched me smash my way out of their protection.

·

In Dad's house I found a little photo of him and Mum in their twenties, sitting on the front step of their first house. Between them lay a long-eared black dog, a spaniel. Dad said his name was Ned. I did not remember our ever having had a pet. I asked if the dog had died before I was born. 'Ah no. I had to get rid of him. Mum wouldn't let him inside. Because of her *brand-new mushroom-pink carpet*.' He laughed, and shrugged. 'I put an ad in the paper. A lady came round and took him. She tied his lead to the carrier of her bike and pedalled away. I thought he might have looked back, but he never even turned his head.'

·

A crime novelist spoke at a conference about the unsuitability of his usual sardonic tone for the war story he was trying to write, 'about young men with their stomachs torn open who cry all night for their mothers and then die'. An old man told me, after he had had open-heart surgery, that he and a ward full of other men his age woke in the dark from hideous nightmares, screaming for their mothers. I have never read or heard of a woman in extremis who called for her mother. It is not possible for me to imagine such a thing. Still, I did hear about a woman of my age who had died in a distant part of the country. Her parents did not go to her funeral. I asked my mother, 'Would you go to my funeral, if I died far away?' She uttered a sharp pant of disbelief. 'If you died in the Arctic *Circle* I'd make m' way there.'

•

On my pantry shelf stands a tall storage jar that I salvaged from Dad's kitchen when we sold his house. It survived the successive demolitions of my mother's households and, I suspect, of her mind. She has labelled it, in her large, clear hand: *Sultanas.* Then she has crossed out *Sultanas* and replaced it with *Currants.* Then she has crossed out *Currants* and restored *Sultanas.* The jar, when I found it, was empty.

•

Her ghost is in my body. I have her long narrow feet with low arches. I have her hollow bones, her hysterectomy, her fading eyebrows, her fine grey-brown hair that resists all attempts at drama. My movements are hers when, on a summer morning, I close up the house against the coming scorcher, or in the evening whisk the dry clothes off the line in weightless armfuls that conceal my face.

In the intermission at *Shane Warne: The Musical* two smiling strangers approached me. The man introduced himself and his wife. Aside from our parents' funerals, I had not seen him since we were children.

'I knew you straightaway,' he said, 'from the other side of the room. You stand exactly like your mother.'

•

In my forties, when I lived in Chippendale, I used to walk to work across the big gardens of Sydney University. I walked fast, thinking my thoughts. One morning a young woman passed me, going the other way. She was wearing an op-shop blouse from the 1940s, striped, with shoulder pads and tiny pearl buttons. At the sight of it a bolt of ecstasy went through me, an atavistic bliss so powerful that its roots could only have been in early childhood. I wrote my mother a letter. Did she ever have a stripy blouse, rather floppy, when I was little?

A week later came a curly edged black-and-white photo. The date pencilled on the back was 1943. A woman in her early twenties stands in a bare backyard, squinting in an unposed way that raises her cheeks and bares her teeth. Her hair is permed and pinned in a victory roll. On her flexed left arm sits a wide-browed, unsmiling baby. The child's right cheek and left hand lean against the stripes of the woman's rayon blouse.

The war is not yet over. Her brother is alive. I am six months old. I am still an only child. She is carrying me in her arms. She is strong enough to bear my weight with ease. I trust her. She is my mother, and I am content to rest my head upon her breast.

2013

Before Whatever Else Happens
DIARY 3

A MAN came to install a shutter on my kitchen window. While he worked, Ambrose wandered in to tell me about a disappointing experience with his schoolmate Hazel, a very spirited little girl, who had come over yesterday to play. 'I tried to kiss her on the trampoline, I tried to hug her, and I tried to dance with her. But she didn't want to be kissed. She didn't want to be hugged. And she didn't want to be danced with.' The shutter bloke downed tools and listened with full attention. 'What grade are you in?' 'Grade two.' The man had a good look at Ambrose, paused, and said quietly, 'Wait a while. That'll change.'

•

Out walking early I spotted a magpie's head over the parapet of a garage. Wind ruffled a feather. I thought, 'That maggie's going to swoop me.' Three seconds later the air stirred above me and a force slashed past my left ear. I let out a screech and waved both arms.

Again it came at me, from behind: the hiss of plumage, the cool rush of air past my cheek.

•

Every day I work on the edit of my book. I slog away, shifting chunks of material and moving them back, eating my salad in a daze, wondering if the linking passages I've written are leading me up a garden path, or are sentimental, or violate some unarticulated moral and technical code I've signed up to and feel trapped in or obliged to. The sheer bloody labour of writing. No one but another writer understands it—the heaving about of great boulders into a stable arrangement so that you can bound up them and plant your little flag at the very top.

•

I keep noticing in the shelf beside my bed the copy of Marcus Aurelius's *Meditations*, a reminder of the wakeful nights I had while I was working on my book. The emperor's thoughts were not much use to me. The Book of Job was more comforting, or Thomas Wyatt: 'I scarce may write, my paper is so wet.'

•

On the train a dark-haired young man in a dirty navy-blue boiler suit and work boots sat beside me. He was holding up a tiny book at eye level, chanting and singing in a very soft voice. It sounded like Arabic, though he didn't seem to be turning the little pages backwards. He was entirely absorbed in his prayers, if that's what they were. I wished I could murmur a psalm with that sort of oblivious devotion.

•

My friend and I came out of *South Pacific* and strode down into Parliament Station in the foolishly lighthearted mood that a musical can induce. A man came stumbling towards us along the tiled concourse, yelling and wailing—barefoot, barelegged, swollen-faced, holding up his pants with both hands, like Poor Tom in *King Lear*. Four tall young policemen were clustering inside the ticket barriers through which he must have been ejected. We swiped our cards and passed through, close to the cops. They were standing in a group, facing each other, half-smiling with a strange awkwardness. One of them, dark and thin and very young, looked shaken by the man's helpless craziness, or perhaps by something he and his fellow officers had done before we got there.

·

To the NGV on St Kilda Road to see a show called 'The Four Horsemen of the Apocalypse'. Dürers, manically detailed and phantasmagorical—tall spires thrusting towards a calm sky through foliage that crouched against a cliff; young lovers surprised by a Grim Reaper behind a tree; a knight clanking past a grave out of which clambered a skeleton. In the dim gallery the woodcuts were exquisite, but fanatical. When I emerged on to the street the world looked frightening and brutal. On the tram a deadbeat with a loud, grating voice praised a little girl's beauty. 'You're gorgeous, you are! Children!' he croaked to her shrinking mother. 'They're a joy, aren't they!' He barged off, cursing the driver, shoving through the crowd. I walked into the house and found the two boys bowed over the computer. I came up behind them on velvet feet, prepared to cut short some monstrous orgy of mayhem. They were intricately manipulating the long red tongue of a frog to catch flies on a lilypad.

·

The boys came to stay the night with me. After dinner I sat on the toilet lid and watched them in the bath: up to their armpits in pale greenish water, talking softly and playing with face washers, wrapping them round their legs in complex bandage shapes. Amby crouched on knees and elbows and I poured bucket after bucket of warm water over his back. Ted, the lofty philosopher, declined my offer, then crept closer and closer until his back and Amby's were touching: 'What about mine?' Soon they were in bed and the house was orderly. The dog lay curled on his pallet outside the back door. A quarter moon blazed very high in an endless warm sky.

•

Werner Herzog's documentary about American prisoners on death row—men found guilty of randomly gruesome crimes which, under the filmmaker's unflinching scrutiny, are suddenly the least interesting things about them. Herzog's Bavarian accent, his almost perfect colloquial American English. To interview his subjects he shoots them from crown of head to hips. After they finish talking he lets long silences fall, but keeps the camera on them, keeps and keeps it on them. Some can tolerate it. Others endure it. Others again lower their eyes, or turn aside. Some go to pieces and start to weep.

•

In Newcastle we had breakfast in a café right on the foreshore at Merewether beach. There was a mild offshore breeze. Great swells bulged and toppled; tiny figures cut across their faces and disappeared in boiling foam. One tousle-haired little teenage surfer called to his friend as they ran down the steps to the sand, 'Hey, Zephyr!' We laughed, thinking he must have hippie parents, but it was more likely short for Zephaniah. What the hell is this fashion for Old Testament boys' names? Regret will come later, as with grandiloquent verbal tattoos.

•

At dinner we play a game of inventing movie ratings. PGF: Parental Guidance Forbidden. TMK: Too Much Kissing. POE: Plenty of Explosions. TSFK: Too Sad For Kids. Ted asks a riddle he says he's just made up: 'What do you call a graveyard that's been cut exactly in half? A symmetry.'

·

Hand-lettered sign in public toilets, Ararat: 'If you're about to use these toilet facilities, we apologise in advance, we know they're not the best.'

·

We drive down to Queenscliff to inspect my parents' graves, which other family members have recently discovered to be looking neglected and unloved, their black lettering faded almost to vanishing point. We enter the bush cemetery expecting a desolate scene, but in fact, among the larger, squarer, darker graves, our parents' pale, curved little vertical headstones, side by side, look modest and rather elegant. From behind they resemble the shoulders of a couple sitting in a theatre waiting for the show to start.

·

Toni Morrison on what her children needed from her as a single mother: 'One, they needed me to be competent. Two, they wanted me to have a sense of humour. And three, they wanted me to be an adult.'

I reckon I scored all right on one and two. Three, not so much. Back then. But there she goes across the yard, my daughter. With her light firm step.

·

A teenager on the 57 tram offers his mate some advice about women.

'Don't give 'em too much attention! They take advantage! Just 'cause you root 'em they think you're gonna go out with 'em!'

·

Ted shows me his school composition, a rewrite of Snow White from the point of view of the dwarves: 'So you think we liked Snow White? You are completely WRONG.'

•

Recovering from pneumonia I spend an afternoon on the couch with Ambrose, watching *Adventure Time*. We laugh, I doze, I wake and doze and laugh again. A cold, dark day. Towards evening I glance out the window at the sodden yard.

    H: 'Oh! The wind blew!'

    A: (in a cynical tone) 'What's so cool about wind blowing?'

    H: 'What's so NOT cool about wind blowing, smartarse?'

•

Home, sobered by the documentary about the wild life and early death of Amy Winehouse, we sit down to dinner. Before we can reach for our forks my granddaughter says in a low voice, 'Could we have a moment's silence? For Amy?' Later, while I wash the pans and serving dishes, she and her mother sit on the couch to sort and fold a huge mound of dry laundry. They watch '100 Top Hits from the '90s', murmuring together about the bands. Once or twice they laugh. Their swift, neat movements, their easy companionship.

•

In the transit lounge at Dubai airport I share a café table with a brick-layer from Frankston: a small, tough, shyly smiling bloke of fifty or so, capable-looking and fit, with weather-beaten skin and faded, old-fashioned tatts. His thick grey hair is cut short and he has a husky, smoker's voice. There is something pained in his face, an openness. He's on his way to Edinburgh, he says, and from there up to the Shetland Islands: 'My wife came from there.'

    'Came?'

    'Yeah. She…passed away. I don't like to say it.'

    'That's hard.'

'We had a very happy marriage. That's why I'm taking the trip.'

'How come you didn't do it together?'

'We bought a holiday house to renovate, and it took up all our time and money. Then she got sick. So I'm going on my own, before whatever else happens.'

We take a walk around the huge bare terminal. In the carpeted aisles men are sound asleep on the floor, in rows, some on mats, some with shirts or scarves drawn over their mouths and noses. Half-a-dozen young men in starched white robes stroll about together. Their bearded faces have an otherworldly, purified look, their eyes are unfocused. One has a length of fine white cloth tossed casually over his head and shoulders. Perhaps they're coming home from Mecca. Every hour or so, during our long wait, a man's soft voice on the PA recites a prayer, or perhaps a blessing. Neither of us remarks on it, but my sad tradie, too, in his pure white T-shirt, is on a pilgrimage.

•

The old American woman sitting next to me on the plane watches me tear an article out of a *Times Literary Supplement*. 'Are you a writer?'

'How can you tell?'

'I'm a psychologist.'

•

A caller on talkback radio says he was on the side of the striking teachers until they announced that they wouldn't write comments on the children's reports. 'That was it,' he barks. 'The minute it started to affect *me*, I was against them.' For a moment even the mouthy radio host is struck dumb.

•

The Trotskyist at the health resort, a pretty woman in her sixties with a cloud of curls, sat forward on the low couch after dinner, elbows across her thighs, and blazed on, unstoppable, about international politics. Her eyes seemed to move closer together and sink deeper into her skull; her lips twitched. She didn't want to hear what we thought. She knew everything. She had read 'thousands of books'. When someone she had interrupted registered a mild protest, she flared up: 'I only started talking about the Middle East because I was *asked questions*!' She contained the truth: she was a vessel filled to the brim with it; the lightest touch or tilt and out it poured—to her a precious nectar, to others a choking flood that drowned whatever frail proposition anyone else came up with.

•

A massage, by a silent young woman with long dark hair in a ponytail and large thoughtful eyes. Towards the end of the hour, while she worked on my right hand, I had a strange vision: that she was not touching me, but standing near me and transferring great armfuls of hydrangea-like flowers from one flat surface to another.

•

'She's one of those women,' says my friend, 'who put on perfume by spraying a cloud and walking into it.'

•

Three scorchers in a row. I went to pick up the boys from school. The sky was clouding over and the air was irritable. I waited at a table in the breezeway. Suddenly, above the asphalt of the big playground came a mighty rushing, counterclockwise, as if the air were being stirred by a spoon in a huge bowl. A blast of dirt hit me side-on. I sprang to my feet and ran to shelter in a stairwell. Grit poured past, heading north. The temperature plummeted and a superb, refreshing cool exploded all around. Raindrops struck the asphalt, stopped, then began in earnest. A teacher ran past. '*I* think it's *great*!' she cried, as if someone had complained. She let out a yell: 'Waaa hoooo!' The bell rang, and hundreds of kids burst out on to the playground, shouting, running, veering wildly and shrieking with laughter, arms extended, bags thumping on their backs. 'The change! The change! The cool change is here!'

•

The nurse took the needle out of my arm and carried away a big flat dark red bag of my blood. I went to a table in the recovery area and prepared to read *Woman's Day* for the regulation fifteen minutes, but soon I broke out in a sweat. My eyes weren't working. Everything was going dotted and speckled. Oh God. I would have to draw attention to myself. I cried out feebly to the world at large, 'Help! I'm going to faint!' Two nurses ran from the other end of the room and grabbed me by the shoulders: 'On to the floor. Get on to the floor.' They laid me out on the lino tiles and fanned me with magazines. They kept asking if I felt better. 'No. Gonna be sick.' One of them put to my mouth a soft little plastic container shaped like a windsock. 'Turn on your side.' I obeyed. Nothing came up, just empty spasms. Loud pop music was playing, songs from the '70s and '80s. Faces came and went above my head, looking down at me without curiosity. The nurses flattened out a padded chair and got me on to it with my head lower than my heart. Water, salty pretzels, rest. In twenty minutes they gave me a cab voucher and someone walked me down the stairs to the Bourke Street cab rank. The driver scowled over his shoulder when I told him my inner-suburban destination: he rudely made it clear that it was not far enough. I bit his head off and told him to get going. A woman who has just sprawled retching on the floor of the Blood Bank is not to be trifled with.

•

'Get crossways of me, LaBoeuf, and you will think a thousand of brick has fell on you.'
    Charles Portis, *True Grit*

•

At an Australian literature conference in Armidale a dozen of us were taken by bus to visit the birthplace of the poet Judith Wright. In a homestead of deep, flowery verandas we were welcomed by female relatives with the long legs and quiet authority of horsewomen, not to mention the ability to knock up an airy sponge cake. While we were standing in the bedroom in which the poet had first seen the light of day, one of the academics murmured, 'I once went into the room where Thomas Hardy was born. They didn't think he'd survive. They threw him into a corner.'

•

She walks in my front door at dinnertime. I've made up the bed and turned on the lamps in her room, put some nasturtiums in a glass, laid out clean towels. Everything is pleasant and welcoming, but she doesn't seem to notice. In the kitchen, where the air is perfumed by the soup I've got warming on the stove, I make the mistake of saying, 'You've got a choice. Chicken and leek soup here, or turkey next door.' Her tired face lights up: 'Turkey?' I suppose my kitchen bench does look a bit spartan, with its one small handful of broccoli on the chopping board.

•

After the public interview a woman came up to me and said without preliminary, in an accusing tone, 'You were nervous.'

H: (surprised) 'No, I wasn't nervous.'

Woman: 'You were *nervous*.'

H: 'I always twitch and jump around in my seat, if that's what you mean.'

Woman: (irritably) 'I didn't mean that. *You—were—nervous*.'

Luckily someone came up and interrupted us before I was obliged to punch her lights out.

•

One wigged and robed barrister to another, barging along William Street: 'And as for this sleazebag fuckin' spinmeister I work for—'

•

A middle-sized bird fell from the sky into our backyard. It was still alive when the boys found it, but one of the chickens, which had recently sprouted shiny purple tail feathers and was on death row, rushed at it and began to maul it. 'Its back was broken,' Ambrose told me, the tears still drying on his cheeks. 'And David got the spade, and he hit it and hit it and hit it, and it went Er, er, er, er, er, er, and then it was dead.' He wanted to write an epitaph. I gave him pencil and paper and he toiled over a draft: 'This is a bird who went into our rooster's territory. With a broken back, the rooster attacked it and then my dad took out his shovel and whacked it to death.' Rather than correct his misattached modifier, I suggested we edit it down to a single sentence. He printed it with thick red texta on a piece of board: 'Here lies a young bird.' We pounded the stake into the grave, and away he ran, singing.

•

'I'd love it,' says the tired wife to the husband, 'if you made me a really nice little martini.' He goes out to the kitchen. We hear the sharp metallic rattle of the shaker. Soon he returns bearing an expert little creation in a dainty glass. He hands it to her in a forward-leaning posture of gentle formality, and she accepts it with a smile. The quality of enchanted light that a martini emits in a lamplit room: icy, misty, strangely and coldly white—she might have been receiving a star, or an atomic particle, and raising it to her lips.

•

The young colourist, silken-haired and soft-voiced, started plastering my head with a thick creamy-yellow paste. 'Don't worry about the colour!' she said. 'It won't look anything like this!' Thirty minutes later she came back and shampooed it out. I looked in the mirror and was so shocked I could hardly speak. My mousy hair was now a dense, unmodulated brown, as if a furry thing had dropped from the beak of a high-flying raptor and landed on my head.

•

I took the heeler to my office, but he couldn't deal with the stairs. He made it up to the first landing, then lost his nerve and lay flat on his belly, quivering and gazing at me imploringly. Somehow I urged him back down the steep staircase: his steps were as mincing as those of a girl in her first high heels. He kept his eyes fixed on his forefeet, each of which splayed as it took his weight.

•

In the cocktail bar the waitress, turning away from our table with her tray, placed her left hand, palm out, flat against the small of her back: a tiny gesture of professional composure. The first time she did it I was touched and wanted to laugh. The second time I felt more like crying, it was so delicate and graceful.

•

David and the kids played a wild game in the kitchen. He stood facing the closed back door and bent over, bracing his arms against the frame. The challenge was for each kid to take a run at him, leap, and kick his arse with both feet while completely airborne. Olive filmed a few attempts on the iPad, then laid it aside and queued for a turn. The rules were very strict and he kept making them stricter. The airborne factor was paramount. The two kicks had to be separate but in rapid succession. You had to take off from the right foot but also deliver the first kick with that same foot. Ted did it perfectly once: we heard his feet connect with David's jeans, whack-whack, the unique flat sound of blows on denim. No one could match it. Everyone was shouting and laughing. When we looked at the little videos they were as dark and mysterious as paintings—David, turning from the door to declare the next rule, made masterful gestures with hands that showed white against his black jumper, and his voice on the faint soundtrack was a series of thick, low quacks.

•

My book is about to be published. I have worked on it for over seven years. To my amazement people keep asking me, before it's even in the shops, 'Have you started something else? What's your next project?' If you must know, I'm planning to lie on my bed for twelve months. Or, as Elena Ferrante says, 'When you've finished a book, it's as if your innermost self had been ransacked, and all you want is to regain distance, return to being whole.'

•

After the birthday party I stayed over at her house. It was a humid Sydney night. A small fan stood at the foot of the mattress I slept on, sending a quiet, steady airstream along me hour after hour. I dreamt I held a creamy little baby close to my chest all night; not my child, but it knew me, trusted me, and consented to sleep in my embrace. In the morning I had to catch an early plane. I slipped out of the house without waking anyone. The pavements were wet. A cab cruised close to me and blinked its lights. I got in. The driver was a young man in a white embroidered cap. He drove in silence through the industrial streets, and the light grew over the city murky with rain, the huge Sydney figs, the frames of new apartment blocks, slender cranes standing motionless among them. Neither of us spoke. Nothing was expected of me and I was grateful.

2015

PART FOUR

On Darkness

Punishing Karen

ONE Tuesday morning in August, a seventeen-year-old secondary student I'll call Karen told her parents that she felt sick and wanted to stay home from school. They assumed she had a cold. But at about four in the afternoon, while her mother was outside washing the car, Karen gave birth, on hands and knees in her own bed, to a full-term baby boy.

She cut the umbilical cord with a pair of scissors. Then she gave the infant several hard punches to the head, wrapped him in a towel, put him on the floor beside her bed, and went into the bathroom to wash. While she was in the shower, her mother, who had not known Karen was pregnant, came back into the house and saw blood in her daughter's bed. Karen said she had a very heavy period, but then her mother found the baby, bundled in his towel. She made up the bed freshly and let Karen sleep for a couple of hours. Then mother and daughter took the baby to hospital, where he was declared dead.

Karen claimed that in her exhaustion after the labour she had collapsed on top of the baby. But when Homicide detectives pointed out that such a fall could not explain the bruising, the haemorrhage and the eight areas of fracture that the autopsy had revealed, she confessed that she had struck the baby several times in the head, intending to kill him, for she did not want to keep him.

The prisoner who faced the judge from the dock at the Victorian Supreme Court was a slip of a girl with long, fine, dark hair, dressed like any teenager in low-slung pants and a cotton top. To hear the charge of infanticide read out against her, to be told that she had managed to conceal her pregnancy for its entire duration, had laboured furtively and in silence, and had delivered the infant alone, staining her girlhood bed with blood—this was terrible enough; but one's mind veered away from the rest, as did one's eyes from her downcast, expressionless, rather handsome profile. When she pleaded guilty to the charge the air in the court was thick with shock and pity.

Karen's counsel sketched out a provincial Australian life poignant in its ordinariness. She was the eldest of three sisters. Her father, whose tough discipline and 'yelling' she feared while longing for his approval, was a fitter. Her mother was a part-time retail assistant. At the time of her baby's birth and death she was in year twelve; she finished the year with a tertiary entrance score of 38.8, and was now studying visual arts at TAFE. She played in a basketball team and worked twenty hours a week in a supermarket. Several friends had accompanied her to court. Twenty-one people from her country town had produced character references.

She had had no further sexual relationships since she broke up with the child's father, an unnamed person whose existence was otherwise never mentioned in the proceedings. Her mother, a kind-faced woman, told the court of her daughter's distraught tears, her remorse, her need for comfort.

How should the court deal with such a girl? The judge's face, one fancied, showed the distress felt by all those present. His brow was creased, his mouth turned down at the corners. The maximum penalty in Victoria for killing a child in the first twelve months of its life (after that, the charge becomes murder) is five years. The very notion of infanticide acknowledges that the balance of a new mother's mind may remain disturbed for many months by the violent physiological changes of childbirth.

Only one expert witness gave evidence at the hearing: a clinician and researcher in the field of post-partum psychiatric illness. The psychiatrist introduced a further refinement: the concept of neonaticide, where a mother kills her baby within twenty-four hours of its birth. It's during the first day of a baby's life, said the witness, that it runs the greatest risk of being murdered. Almost half of the girls who conceal their pregnancy will kill their baby.

In many of these girls, the knowledge of the pregnancy never reaches a conscious level. Karen knew all right, but she 'kept squashing the knowledge down'. She was childlike, said the psychiatrist, with little insight, poor judgment and few planning skills. She sought no antenatal care or advice, she didn't consider an abortion. She 'just kind of hoped it would all go away'. But in the panic and terror of giving birth alone, she entered a brief state of dissociative psychosis in which she killed the baby. Even the Crown offered no objection to this interpretation.

What is bewildering about these stories, and almost every woman knows of one, at second or third hand, is not only why a girl hides her pregnancy but how. How can her family, her intimates, fail month after month to see the obvious? Karen's mother told the court that she had 'suspected' it when her daughter appeared to be putting on weight; but once Karen had denied it, she asked no further questions. It's as if a girl's iron refusal of her state can induce in others a sort of hysterical blindness.

It has been suggested by psychologists and anthropologists that most neonaticides remain undiscovered—that neonaticide is wired into humans, and that our disinclination to imprison these young mothers, and our pity for their plight, points to our unexpressed sense that newborns have not yet reached full human status.

Researchers say that girls' will to deny pregnancy can be so powerful that they suppress the symptoms. They can give birth within earshot of other people, and not cry out; some even say they felt no pain. Some, when they return to awareness and find the dead infant, have no idea how it got there. Babies are found under beds, in cupboards, shoved into bags. One young woman put her dead baby into a filing cabinet that she shared with others at her office.

'My guess,' the psychiatrist told the court, 'is that if Karen's mother hadn't come in and found the baby, Karen would have just left him there. Even to try to hide him would be to face that it had happened.'

When the court resumed that afternoon for sentencing, the girl sat in the dock, frozen faced.

'Karen,' said the judge. 'Would you stand up? I am not going to send you to jail.' A tremor passed along her lips. 'You know that jails are nasty, violent places. All of the purposes of punishment can be achieved without putting you in jail.' He gave her a three-year good behaviour bond on condition that she continue to see a counsellor. 'But if you fall foul of the law, you'll be brought back here and sentenced to imprisonment. Do you understand?'

She opened her mouth and uttered a tiny, strangled squeak of assent.

'Come down here, Karen, and sign the undertaking.' She obeyed, then made as if to return to the dock.

'You don't have to go back there,' said the judge gently. 'Go and sit with your mother.'

As the court rose, Karen's father put one arm around her and held her close against his side.

Scarcely out of childhood, the girl had gone through an ordeal so unimaginable that even the thought that she had killed a helpless infant with her fists could not make people want to punish her. She left the court shielded by her parents, with her sister and friends clustering behind. They crossed William Street in a tight phalanx. Cameramen backed away in front of them. Karen kept her head low, but later, on the TV news, one could discern in her face, through the screen of her hair, the faintest trace of softening, though nothing as free as a smile.

2005

The Singular Rosie

ONE hot afternoon in February 2014, in the pleasant Victorian township of Tyabb, south-east of Melbourne, an eleven-year-old boy called Luke Batty was playing in the nets after cricket practice with his father, Greg Anderson. Without warning, Anderson swung the bat and dealt the child a colossal blow to the back of his head, then crouched over him where he lay, and attacked him with a knife. The police shot Anderson and he died in hospital the following morning.

Rosie Batty, the young boy's mother, came out her front gate to address the media. Her thick fair hair was tangled, her face stripped raw. 'I want to tell everybody,' she said to camera, in a low, clear voice with a Midlands accent, 'that family violence happens to everybody. No matter how nice your house is, how intelligent you are. It can happen to anyone, and everyone. This has been an eleven-year battle. You do the best you can. You're a victim, and you're helpless. An intervention order doesn't stop anything like this from happening.'

It wasn't so much what she said as her demeanour that stopped people in their tracks. There was something splendid about her, in her quiet devastation. Everyone who saw her was moved, and fascinated. People talked about her with a kind of awe.

The night before I visited Rosie Batty, in July, I had a dream. I found myself in a house with her and several other Englishwomen, broad-browed and composed, like characters in a George Eliot novel. Their faces were swollen and stark, as if they had been swimming in grief for an eternity. But there was at the same time a gentleness in the room, a mysterious patience—a sense that the women's pain was not the only thing that existed in their world; that they knew this, and that they were prepared to trust the knowledge. By the time I had spent a day with the real Rosie, the singular Rosie, I understood that the quality people found so impressive in her was not merely the authority of the brutally bereaved, but also this wisdom, this trust.

Rosie Batty lives on a small green acreage on the outskirts of Tyabb. In her paddocks goats wander. Donkeys utter their strange cries. We sat by her living room fire all afternoon with a young dog lying on the mat between us. Rosie is lively company: a straight-talking, irreverent and very funny woman of fifty, a self-mocking mimic who really knows how to tell a story.

The care she was offered during the time after Luke's death was very taxing to the independent soul of someone who lost her mother when she was six, and who had lived as a single mother for years.

'I spent two days on the couch,' she said. 'I don't think I even got changed. I didn't want to go into my bed because Luke used to sleep with me there. I was basically comatose on the couch. A lot of wonderful people came to help me, but soon they started trying to make decisions for me. "Oh, Rosie, you can't go out to the media! You mustn't!" I had to keep saying, "If I need your help, I won't have any problem asking." One hug's all right, but I had to say, "Do not keep touching me! Do not keep trying to embrace me!" And somebody was always vacuuming or blowing leaves around. The noise! It got into my brain and I lost it—"*What the fuck are you doing?*"'

More to her taste was the old and dear friend who phoned her after she had appeared on TV looking slightly unkempt. 'He said, "Clean yourself up, woman. You look like shit."'

Then a Homicide detective came round to tell her that somebody really important wanted to call her that evening.

'Bruce Springsteen was touring,' Rosie told me, 'and I'd been supposed to go to his concert. It's low of me, isn't it, but I thought to myself, I love Bruce Springsteen. Maybe he might get to know my story and give me a call.'

The very important caller, announced the detective, was the prime minister, Tony Abbott.

'I went, "Ahhh!", but inside I was thinking, Oh, *damn.*'

In the months since Luke was murdered, Rosie Batty has become an advocate for victims of domestic violence, speaking publicly about her frustrating experiences with the government bodies whose job it is to protect women and children. She did not scruple to shout at a callow TV presenter who made sanctimonious pronouncements about mandatory reporting. She is working hard with the lawyers who are preparing a brief for the coronial inquest into Luke's death, slated for mid-October. When the Commission for Children and Young People announced at a directions hearing in August that its report would not be ready in time for the inquest, she spat the dummy outside the Coroner's Court. Bureaucrats ducked for cover. Like many a bereaved mother, she has lost all fear of people in power. She has an unerring bullshit detector, which she applies equally to her own public persona. 'I have to be careful,' she said to me, with her wry grin, 'that my little halo doesn't slip down and strangle me.'

Rosie had never intended to have a child. But when she found herself pregnant at nearly forty, during a brief rekindling of an affair with her former workmate Greg Anderson, she went ahead. Anderson was an intelligent but prickly and rather rigid man with a lot of peculiar religious and philosophical ideas that he liked to argue about, but he could be fun, and she had always liked the way he was not intimidated by her. By the time Luke was born they had parted for good, but Anderson was keen to have some involvement with the child, and when he came round, Rosie was grateful for his practical help. Photos of him holding Luke show the baby's tiny fist locked around the tall man's forefinger, the father gazing down, rapt.

Throughout Luke's childhood, Anderson came and went. 'Every time I relaxed my boundaries,' said Rosie, 'I'd bloody pay for it. There was always a trigger. Something would happen that made him feel inadequate, and he'd start again with his character assassination of me. He was a big, proud man who couldn't have his own way.'

Anderson's life began to fall apart. He became abusive and impossible in work situations, and could not keep even a manual job. He thought he was too clever for other people: he was possessed by a warped vanity, a tendency to contempt and scorn. He wound up jobless and unemployable, at times even living in his car. Once or twice he asked Rosie if he could store stuff in her shed, and she agreed, because she pitied him. He would send her the occasional offensive email or text, talking about dark energy and telling her how evil she was, but in the end she got irritated and bored. 'I would just think, *Oh, fuck off.* Over the years I got used to him being odd and saying ridiculous things. I'd say, "You know what? You're not dragging me into your world." The only thing I could control was how I let him affect me. People would say, "He's going to ruin your life," and I'd say, "No, he's *not*. Ultimately he's in it, because he's Luke's dad, and I can't do anything about that. But I have *quality of life*." Back then I hadn't understood that there are different forms of violence.'

Rosie began to think she had Anderson figured out, that she knew how to handle his weird, aggressive behaviour, which was always aimed at her, never at their son. She let it roll over her, and carried on. Despite this tedious black cloud, she and Luke lived the peaceful rural life she had always wanted to provide for him, with neighbours and friends, a happy school, sporting clubs, all their animals.

Through his misfortunes, Anderson's love for Luke never wavered. On his visits he was kind and patient with the little boy, and they loved to play together. But one day Luke came home from an outing and told Rosie that in the car his father had said he was tired of this life, and wished he could go into the next one. He had shown Luke a knife and said, 'It could all end with this.' A court order stopped his access to the boy. Anderson challenged the order. Under pressure, Rosie compromised: the court decided that Anderson would be allowed to see Luke only in public places, when he was playing sport. Soon after this, the Victorian Child Protection Service effectively closed Luke's case.

Rosie took Luke to England for Christmas 2013 with her family. By the time they got back to Australia, there were four police warrants out for Anderson's arrest. Rosie knew nothing of this. Information that might have been a red flag for her, as Anderson's mental state darkened, was withheld from her on privacy grounds. No one told her that he had been taken in for looking at child pornography at a public library, or that he had threatened to cut off the head of a fellow resident of his share house. So on the afternoon of 12 February 2014, when she and Luke arrived at the local cricket ground for practice and Anderson came towards them 'with a big smile', warning bells did not go off. When Luke ran up to her at the end of the session and asked if he could have a few extra minutes of play at the nets with his dad, because they were having so much fun, she was glad to give permission, and off he ran.

The architecture of Rosie Batty's face may be monumental, but the air around her is so clear that one can ask her anything.

'Are you religious?'

'I was raised in the Church of England,' she said. 'But in my early twenties I started to read books. I didn't read fiction for years. I started with people like Deepak Chopra and Louise L. Hay. Then I found stuff about spirituality and Buddhism.'

'Do you find those things any use to you now?'

'Yes, I do. Taking responsibility. We're here on our own individual journey...'

She sounded vague. Perhaps she was getting tired. She changed position on the couch and tried again, leaving very long pauses, sometimes holding her breath and letting it out in soft, voiceless gasps.

'I believe that we're here to be tested. To have life lessons. To enhance all the qualities of compassion and empathy and love. To grow. The only other choice is—if you can't grow, you're gonna shrivel. So there isn't a choice, really. You seek to grow, no matter what happens that may debilitate you for a time. But it's in you to keep growing. To keep rising up, and learning something from it. And surging forward. Some people can't. Or won't. They stay bitter, or angry. Or try to dull their pain. They stay blaming other people.'

'Where's Luke now?' I said. '*What's* Luke, now?'

She drew a vast sigh, and said with great firmness and certainty, 'If there is an afterlife, he will be in a blessed place.'

'Where's his father, then?'

'I have to remind myself,' she said, choosing her words delicately, 'that Greg died too. I didn't ever want him to suffer. The best thing that could happen was for him to be…removed. He was such a tormented man. He believed the worst of everybody. It was exhausting. I don't think of him a lot. He's just dropped away. All my thoughts and emotions are consumed with Luke. With losing him. With what I'm not going to be able to share with him.' She took several long breaths. 'Or see.'

We sat there in silence. The dog slept on between us. Rosie rested her forearms across her thighs and turned her grand, weary face up to me.

'Sometimes,' she said, 'it gets so quiet. And I think, *what's missing?*' Her voice weakened and trembled. 'I know what's missing. What's missing is Luke. Was he ever here?'

2014

they had CCTV in that bridal shop. Did you go to the march? I was worried that it would be too peaceful, not enough about how women aren't safe to walk home alone. I was more worried that people would start screeching about civil rights violations. How can the streets ever be made safe? There's evil in the world. The place where she was dumped is out near Vanessa's. Would you go there? No way. It looked beautiful on TV. Soft. Long grass blowing in the wind. And in the foreground you could see a disturbed patch. Imagine being a cop and walking towards that shallow grave. It was *shallow*. He must have just scraped some dirt over her and bolted. Do you think he thought it was worth it? Does a bloke like that *think?* Would he have been trying for years to keep a grip? Did you hear that on the CCTV tape he puts out his hand as if to touch her cheek? And she rears back? I heard that another woman came forward with a story from a year ago. Some guy had tried to persuade her to get into his car. She got away. But she said he had a pitch. A pitch? What's that mean? It's when they sound plausible enough to make you pause in your stride and pay attention. Just long enough for them to gain a psychological advantage. I nearly went down to the court. But I thought it would be too horrible. In the police car, when he was doubled over with his hands clasped behind his neck, you could see he was wearing a wedding ring. No, he had a ring on every finger. What about the poor guy, her workmate, who offered to walk her home? And she said no, she'd be all right? I feel so bad for him. All the women he's ever known would be feminists. He would have learnt not to patronise them with his protectiveness. God, how many times have I walked home feeling invincible. In the '60s Evie used to stroll across Fawkner Park at midnight. She said she was never scared. Yeah, but she was tall. So? I wish I'd gone to the march. Do you think the flowers and candles in Sydney Road were a bit melodramatic? I saw some women crossing themselves. As if it was a shrine. Well, it was, and at least the flowers were fresh, and not wrapped in horrible plastic like the ones people left in London for Princess Di. It's spring, I suppose, flowers everywhere. Princess Di happened in summer. I was on a train in France a few days after the crash. A Frenchwoman saw me reading about it in the paper. She said, 'Can you explain to me this immoderate mourning?' Do you think the Jill Meagher demo was immoderate? That idea keeps coming to me, but I scotch it—I hate the way it makes me feel cynical and ironic. Why didn't you go? I tried. Someone said it was at noon on Saturday. I stuck some rosemary in my buttonhole and drove up to the corner of Moreland Road. I thought there'd be fifty or a hundred people but there was nobody. Only a few women in headscarves doing their shopping. There was a cold wind. Everything was grey and desolate. I hung around for a while, and went home. Then on Sunday night I saw it on the news. I couldn't believe it. Thirty thousand people. Sydney Road packed solid for miles. You should have gone on Facebook, idiot. I don't know how to—I'm stuck in a pre-Facebook world. Some people are saying the whole thing was only a social media phenomenon. Who cares? I was sad. I wanted to be around other people who were sad. Actually I howled. Me too. I've been sick about it all week. My guts were in a knot. I kept tripping over things and bumping into walls.

We gave up on the bar with its thundering men and parted on Bourke Street. On the platform at Parliament Station I read while I waited. A man sat down beside me. I glanced up. He was in his thirties, dark jaw, dark brow. Holding out his iPhone in cupped hands, he shuffled his bum along the bench until our sides touched. I leaned away.

'Excuse me,' he said. His face was shining. 'I hope you don't mind. I've come from the hospital. My wife's just had our first child, a few hours ago. Can I share it with you?'

The Man in the Dock

THE man in the dock looks like someone you wouldn't want to meet in a dark alley. His hair is cropped to the skull. He has a pale, bony face, with long cheeks, still eyes, and sculpted lips that from time to time he purses. His name, let's say, is John Kennedy. He is twenty-seven. He has spent the last two years on remand waiting to be tried for manslaughter, but he has agreed to plead guilty to a lesser charge: reckless conduct endangering life. The most he can get for this is ten years. By forgoing a jury trial, Kennedy is throwing himself on the mercy of a judge.

One winter evening in 2010, he was drifting round Melbourne's CBD with a bunch of street kids known to the Department of Human Services and to the police. They wandered down to the Yarra, to drink and horse about on a concrete pontoon under the pedestrian bridge that links Flinders Street Station with Southbank. One of the girls went behind a pylon with a sixteen-year-old African refugee who had been removed from his parents' care, against their wishes, by the DHS. While they were having sex, the girl let out a scream.

Kennedy ran to them. 'I'm gonna push this cunt,' he said, and gave the boy a one-handed shove in the chest. There was no railing. The boy fell backwards into the river. He could not swim. Several hours later, divers found his body lying on the riverbed, in two metres of murky water.

A sentencing hearing is a quiet, careful process, a conversation between judge and counsel that offers little drama to a casual observer. Yesterday the judge, a woman of famously unbending will, expelled Kennedy's female friends for taking photos of him on their phones. Today the body of the court is empty but for four male lawyers, three women journalists, a dozen students upstairs, and a solidly built young woman with long, unwashed hair and a pugnacious expression, who is seated directly below the dock, with her arms folded and her back to the prisoner. Glances of curiosity she repels with a bulldog glare.

The death of the young refugee, says the judge, is tragic. Judge and counsel deplore the awful irony that the boy should have fled a war-torn country and perished here as he did. His death is certainly relevant to the sentencing. But the prisoner is not charged with that. He is charged with conduct endangering life. There is no evidence that he knew the teenager couldn't swim. He is not to be punished for the death.

The unfenced pontoon was a disaster waiting to happen, but there's a limit, says the judge tartly, to how much people can be protected; and anyway, going by the documents before her, Kennedy himself is a travelling disaster. His father bolted before he was born. His mother died of septicaemia. He is intellectually slow and has been a client of Disability Services since 1989. At eighteen he had a fifteen-year-old girlfriend and was registered as a sexual offender. In 2008 he fell from a roof and was in intensive care for three weeks. Since his brain injury, his mental function has dropped 'from a pretty low base' into the bottom one per cent of the population. He has a long criminal history of violence, and a tendency to become aggressive with very little provocation.

Kennedy sits quietly in the dock, making occasional grimaces with his lips, seemingly unaffected by this alarming description. The long-haired woman sitting in front of him keeps her scowling gaze on the judge's face.

What, asks the judge, is the court to *do* with this man? She is obliged to think about the protection of the community. Locking him up is no solution. But his violence is ongoing and escalating. He needs something other than just prison, something that will help him. But he breaches community orders. He breaches parole.

'I'm not saying that's flash,' says his counsel morosely. He asks permission to call the day's sole witness. Everyone looks at the door. But instead, the scowling woman seated near the dock leaps to her feet and charges eagerly along the carpeted aisle to the witness stand. Up the steps she bounds, seizes the Bible and takes the oath in a clear, ringing voice.

She is the prisoner's penpal, his future partner. She has almost completed a Bachelor of Education at Victoria University. She began to correspond with Kennedy at the suggestion of a friend whose boyfriend was also in prison. 'I had just come out of a three-year relationship,' she gabbles, panting, tripping over her words.

The judge props both elbows on the bench. 'No hurry,' she says. 'Take a deep breath.'

The young woman smiles up at her. She grips the edge of the witness stand, draws in and releases a huge, audible breath.

'I was reluctant at first,' she says, 'because I didn't want to get hurt again.'

First they wrote letters. She got herself on to the list of people he was allowed to telephone. She started to visit him at Port Phillip on Thursdays, when people can see prisoners in protective custody.

'And now,' she says, with a proud little laugh, 'he calls me five or six times a day!'

No, he has never behaved towards her with aggression, let alone violence. Well, yes, of course they have never actually been together; we're talking supervised prison visits here—but no, she has never been afraid of him. Yes, she has met his 'family unit', the suburban household into which he will be accepted when he is released, and she has found it 'appropriate: as far as I'm aware, she's his auntie. She's supposed to be his mother's sister.' The young woman is determined to maintain contact with her own 'family unit', though; she is not stupid.

'And,' she declares, squaring her shoulders and straightening her spine, 'I have made it abundantly clear that I have a clean criminal record, and that I will not tolerate living in the presence of someone who's going to continue to break the law.'

Kennedy sits there, working his lips. He has certainly had 'an unfortunate life'. He has badly hurt people, and now someone has died because of him. The judge will not sentence him today; she will go away and think about it. But for now she listens, chin on palm, with a genial, patient attention, her wig low on her brow, the corners of her scarlet mouth curving upwards. Like her, every person here trembles for the witness, this brave, foolish, big-bosomed girl in her white blouse and chipped nail polish, the girl who wants to love and to be needed, and who is offering to go in, carrying all our hope and dread, where justice fears to tread.

2012

On Darkness

LAST year I published *This House of Grief,* a book about the trials of a Victorian man Robert Farquharson, who was found guilty of drowning his three young sons in revenge against his former wife. When the book came out I was struck by the number of interviewers whose opening question was 'What made you interested in this case?' It always sounded to me like a coded reproach: was there something weird or peculiar about me, that I would spend seven years thinking about a story like this?

I would slave away in these interviews, trying to come up with sophisticated explanations for my curiosity, but after a while I got tired of being defensive. A man, I thought, loves his three sons. His heart is broken when his wife falls in love with another man and ends their marriage. A year later he's driving the boys home to their mother after a Father's Day outing. His car swerves into a deep dam. He fights his way out of the sunken car, hitches a ride to his ex-wife's place and announces to her that he's killed the kids. He tells everyone that he had a coughing fit and blacked out at the wheel. His ex-wife flatly refuses to believe he drove into the water on purpose. She passionately asserts his innocence at the trial. He is found guilty and gets three life sentences with no parole. He appeals his conviction. The appeal is successful, and he is given a retrial. But by the time he faces court again, his ex-wife has turned against him. She is the volatile witness from hell, so wild and fearless that she makes the court quake.

What's not interesting about that?

People seem more prepared to contemplate a book about a story as dark as this if the writer comes galloping out with all moral guns blazing. A friend of mine told me that the woman who runs his local bookshop had declared she would under no circumstances read my book. Surprised, he asked why. 'Because,' she replied, 'I know that nowhere in the book does she say that Robert Farquharson is a monster.'

If he *had* been a monster, I wouldn't have been interested in writing about him. The sorts of crimes that interest me are not the ones committed by psychopaths. I'm interested in apparently ordinary people who, under life's unbearable pressure, burst through the very fine membrane that separates our daylight selves from the secret darkness that lives in every one of us.

Back in 2000 I was still living in Sydney. My third and last marriage had crashed and burned eighteen months before. I was in a very poor state, emotionally and psychologically. I lived by myself on the fifth floor of an apartment block on top of a hill. Its windows had so much air and light outside them that I was constantly drawn to lean my elbows on the sill. I would look out across the golf course with its lines of massive dark green trees, and its hoses sprinkling bridal veils of spray, and further east, the ruled blue-grey line of the sea beyond Bondi. Some days, though, I couldn't help looking straight down to the well-placed concrete retaining wall directly beneath me, five storeys below. There were days when it seemed wiser not to go near the windows.

Even work was no use to me; I was paralysed. I had spent months in Canberra at the trials of the two women who had been charged with the murder of a young civil engineer called Joe Cinque. One had got ten years (she served four) for manslaughter; the other had been found to have no case to answer. The families of the two young women, and the women themselves, had politely but firmly refused my approaches. I had already conducted long and painful interviews with Joe Cinque's parents, and in doing so had entered into a dangerous relationship of trust with these two suffering people. I had a mass of material to work with but it was all one-sided, hopelessly unbalanced. I was drowning in it. I had no idea how to write the book. I didn't have a commanding place to stand; I didn't yet have the right voice to tell the story of what had been done to Joe Cinque.

Around that time I heard there was a place in Sydney, down near Circular Quay, called the Justice and Police Museum. I read in the paper that a curious new curator had gone up into the roof or down into a cellar and come upon a forgotten cache of old black-and-white photographic negatives. A series of crime-scene photos from the 1940s, '50s and '60s had been developed and presented in a small exhibition. I could not get there fast enough.

Since that first public opening of the archive, many more photos from its fabulous trove have been resurrected and displayed. Certain mug shots have become famous, even hip: there are books of them, you can buy them on postcards. They are striking evocations of period, and of class—precious historical documents. The most popular ones are full-length portraits, unceremoniously shot and unintentionally very beautiful, of men and women who have just been taken into police custody. They front the camera, unsmiling—racy, sinister types, alarmingly worldly or damaged, with a Weimar Republic sort of loucheness in their demeanour. They stand defiantly, chins high, in their pointed strappy shoes and felt hats and unbuttoned wool coats, in the bare stone courtyard of a police station.

At the turn of the millennium, though, when I first slunk into the Justice and Police Museum, there was something discreet, almost tentative about the show. Many of the pictures were free-floating; they had been unearthed minus any identifying material. Some of the most dramatic images contained no human figures at all. A blighted street corner; the scarred door of a warehouse; an overgrown track curving down towards a river; a bedroom of grim poverty, with a candlewick bedspread on a sagging mattress and cracked lino on the floor; a dingy hotel room whose open window, its cheap lacy curtain lifting on an invisible breeze, looks straight on to a brick wall. Where are the people? What has happened here? The photos don't say. The police photographers didn't fancy themselves as artists. Their job was to record what was in front of them, and they did it with a fidelity to duty that sometimes, in its utter lack of rhetorical ornament or self-importance, can reach us, lifetimes later, as an impersonal, manly tenderness.

The photo that haunts me most, though, from the show I saw in 2000, did have a plaque beside it: it stated that a young woman had committed suicide in a cave, in the Blue Mountains. As a viewer, you stand at the cave's mouth looking in. On a rock shelf just inside, the woman has placed her handbag and an ominous-looking black bottle. Her dropped shoes lie on their sides. But where is *she*? You scan the surface of the photo in vain. Then you spot her face, tiny as a coin, far from you in the depths of the cave. She's taken all her clothes off, to die. She's lying on the ground as if asleep, her hair drawn back off her brow and her head turned to the light. She's a figure from a timeless mythological world—a strange, slender, naked little cave-dwelling nymph.

I treasure the memory of this photo because of the purity of the recording eye: its respect for the deep calm of a place where a person has died, or been murdered, or has killed herself; its reverence for what I would even call the holiness of a place where something unthinkable and final has happened. Such a place, if you can bear to stand there, is imbued with a rich and sacred meaning.

I see now that for some years already I had been trying to turn myself into the sort of person who could look steadily at such things, without flinching or turning away. I remember how my friends reacted when I begged them to come with me and look at the photos at the Justice and Police Museum: most of them really did not want to see them; they couldn't understand why I thought they were beautiful. But I knew I could learn from them. So I went back, again and again, usually on my own. I longed to mimic in my own work the brutal simplicity of the police photographs.

I belong to a reading group. We wanted to get real about mighty works of literature. We started with *Paradise Lost*. Then we tackled Homer. This year we're working our way into Virgil's *Aeneid*. Whenever the story explodes into bloodshed, one of the women in the group, an experienced and respected journalist, is assailed by fits of laughter that she can't muffle or control. The rest of us have learnt to pay no attention. We calmly go on reading, taking it in turns around the ring, and in a while she gets a grip, returns to herself and takes her part again. It's actually quite endearing. We don't even comment on it any more. It's her defence against the wild, ancient darkness of what we're reading.

Human beings have many shields against the darkness. A woman is raped, or murdered, and the old cry goes up. What was she doing out on the street alone in the middle of the night? Women shouldn't take short cuts through parks on their way to work, or go running along the riverbank with headphones on. These official warnings drive women crazy because they seem to proceed from an enraging assumption that the public space belongs to men, and that women have no claim on it: we broach it at our peril. But I've come to think that the subtext of what the politicians and police chiefs are saying, in their clumsy, poker-faced way, is this: no matter what the political rhetoric is, please do not assume that because you *should* be safe in public spaces you *will* be safe. There is no way that we can police the world and guarantee your safety. We are as helpless as you against the darkness.

Why are we ever surprised by the scorched earth around a broken family? Our laws and strictures and conventions have no purchase on the dark regions of the soul into which we venture when we love. In the Farquharson trials, people would passionately protest, 'But he loved those boys!' Again and again it surfaced, the sentimental fantasy that love is a condition of simple benevolence, a tranquil, sunlit region in which we are safe from our own destructive urges. But everybody knows that love is brutal. A thousand songs tell the story. Love tears right through to the centre of us, into our secret self, and lays it wide open. Surely Sigmund Freud was right when he said, 'We are never so defenceless against suffering as when we love.'

What people find really hard to bear is the suggestion that they themselves might contain their share of human darkness, hidden inside their souls. I believe this refusal lies behind the strange hostility I encountered, many times, when I was trying to write about Robert Farquharson's trials. Friends would ask me what I was working on. When I told them, they would be at first quite curious—what's he like? What sort of man is he? I would be barely three sentences into an account of his family background, his broken marriage and his broken heart, when my questioner's mouth would harden into a straight line and she would make a sharp stabbing movement at my chest with a straight forefinger and say, angrily, 'You're making excuses!'

There's a term that would often come up at this point in the conversation. A man like Farquharson, some people declared, is evil. That's all he is. He is no longer a person. Neither he nor his crime deserves our attention. 'He was found guilty by two juries,' one woman said to me. 'What else is there to say? I don't want to hear any more about him.' Sometimes I tried to argue. More often I backed away with my tail between my legs. But I kept thinking, and I still think, that there are thousands of men like Farquharson out there—hard-working, tongue-tied Australian blokes who don't understand why their wives got sick of them and turfed them out; dull men whose hearts are broken by rejection and by the loss of their children, and who can't even begin to articulate their pain and rage. Men like these can be dangerous. Isn't that worth thinking about?

Over the seven years of the Farquharson trials I was obliged to develop my own set of defences against the darkness. I had thought of myself as mature and thick-skinned enough to handle it. I never did what I saw some of the more battle-hardened journalists do while witnesses wept and writhed under cross-examination—they would fill out a crossword under the desk, or read the footy pages, or furtively clip their fingernails, or doodle a page full of graves. Like everyone else in the court I allowed myself at certain moments to shed tears or to put my head down on my arms for a moment's relief. But at times I found my reasoning powers cracking under the strain. It wasn't till the trials were over and I started to write the book that I could acknowledge these states:

> Was there a form of madness called court fatigue? It would have mortified me to tell the girl who sat beside me about the crazy magical thinking that filled my waking mind and, at

night, my dreams: if only Farquharson could be found not guilty, then the boys would not be dead. Their mother would drive home from the court and find them playing kick-to-kick in the yard…I could not wait to get home each evening, to haul my grandsons away from their Lego and their light sabres, to squeeze them in my arms until they squirmed. Young boys! How can such wild, vital creatures die? How can this hilarious sweetness be snuffed out, snatched away forever?

It seemed fitting, and in a bizarre way almost consoling, that it was a woman who finally got deep enough into the dam, that night, to find the sunken car. She was Senior Constable Rebecca Caskey of the Search and Rescue Squad. The vehicle, they had calculated, was wedged nose-down in the mud, twenty-eight metres from the bank, in seven and a half metres of water. Testimony so terrible demands a simple telling:

> Caskey dived again. In the mud at the bottom, working blind, she felt her way to what she guessed was the driver's side of the vertical car.
>
> 'The first thing I noticed on the driver's side was an open door, just above the level of my head. Its window was closed. I felt around the edge of the door.'
>
> Again, eyes shut and palms exposed, she mimed her fumbling search.
>
> 'And then,' she said, 'I felt, slightly protruding from the car, a small person's head.'
>
> On the witness stand she cupped both hands before her face, and delicately moved an imaginary object sideways.
>
> 'I pushed it back in. And I shut the door.'…

Soon after midnight Caskey clambered out of the water for the last time. A police 4WD winched the Commodore to the edge of the dam, and a commercial towtruck dragged it, still full of water, up on to the bank. Caskey had been in the dam for several hours. She was cold. She was keen to get changed and go home. Before she left, she took a quick look into the car. She saw three children. Two were in the back. Lying in the front was the one whose head she had touched and, for a moment, held in her hands.

At this point, in an earlier draft of the book, there was another paragraph and it went like this:

> The diver's detachment was exemplary; but had she been pressed for more detail, her composure might have cracked, and then we would all have been lost. Her simple gravity was the only thing holding us back from uttering a great communal howl of horror and grief.

I cut that paragraph. A writer friend of mine made me do it. I remember it hurt me to cut it; my own urge to utter such a howl was almost beyond my control. But in the spirit of the diver, and of those police photographers who disciplined themselves in the face of death and plainly, purely recorded the facts as they saw them, I scribbled out my fancy flourish, and now I'm glad I did.

I saw what the police went through in the course of these trials, and I wanted to emulate what was calm and shrewd and decent in them. Last month I turned on the TV news and saw that a Sudanese woman in an outer western suburb of Melbourne had driven her four kids under six into a lake; three of them had drowned. I confess that my first thought was for the furious, exhausted cops in the Major

Collision Investigation Unit, the ones who barrel out at all hours of the day or night to road smashes where people have died or suffered life-threatening injuries. I longed to get in touch with them, I don't know why—what on earth could I say to them? All the ones I got to know around the court are gone now, anyway, transferred or promoted or burnt out; and the detective with the silver buzz cut, who sat with me under the plane trees up the top of Bourke Street one day and gossiped quietly and gently—what would I say to *him*? I admire you? I pity you? I respect you? No—I *envy* you—because your job is to get into your car and drag yourself out to the scene and try to *do something about it*—while all I can do is sit here on the couch in front of the TV with stupid tears running off my cheeks, unable to form a coherent thought or even to locate in myself an emotion with a name.

In Farquharson's first trial, the Crown screened what they called the submergence videos: the police had fitted up a Commodore like Farquharson's with internal lights and video cameras. They had lowered the car into a dam with a crane, and filmed what it did and what the water did and whether it was possible for a driver to open the door of a sinking car in the way Farquharson said he had. These videos were shown to the court after the police diver had given her restrained testimony about gently pushing Jai Farquharson's body back into the car at the bottom of the dam.

When court rose after that horrible screening the jury looked older, weary and sad. Men's brows were furrowed, women stowed sodden handkerchiefs. People staggered out into the street white-faced.

On the long slow escalator down to Flagstaff station, I could not block out of my mind those small bodies, the tender reverse-midwifery of the diver. The only way I could bear it was to picture the boys as water creatures: three silvery, naked little sprites, muscular as fish, who slithered through a crack in the car's rear window and, with a flip of their sinuous feet, sped away together into their new element.

There's no point roaming around looking for comfort, or so I have found. Comfort is like grace. You can't earn it, or deserve it. You have to thrash on, bearing things as best you can, and hold yourself receptive for the moments when it comes to you of its own accord.

Towards the end of the second Farquharson trial, during breaks in the proceedings when the court was cleared, I used to walk up and down the great bare Victorian corridors of the old Supreme Court, stretching my legs, trying to get the blood moving.

One day I heard what sounded like music, very faint and far away. I thought I was hallucinating, and kept walking. But every time I passed the entrance to a certain west-running hallway, the same thing would happen: fragile drifts of notes and slow arpeggios, as if a ghost in a curtain-muffled room were playing a piano. I was too embarrassed to ask if anyone else had heard it; was I starting to crack up? But one day when there was no one else around I went in search of it. I found that an intersection of two corridors had been roofed in glass or perspex. Two benches had been placed against a wall, and from a tiny speaker, fixed high in a corner, came showering these delicious droplets of sound. It was a resting place that some nameless benefactor had created, for people who thought they couldn't go on.

One afternoon in a different hallway a lady came out of an unmarked office carrying a flat dish. She saw me sitting waiting in the corridor on my own, and approached, holding the plate out in front of her: 'Hello. We've just had a little party and we've got some cakes left over. Would you like a lamington?'

These random incidents seem so strange to me now, such unexpected moments of blessing, that I wonder if I dreamt them. Dreams do come: the unconscious works in us and for us, unceasing, with its saving complexity and its deep knowingness.

Sometimes it seems to me that, in the end, the only thing people have got going for them is imagination. At times of great darkness, everything around us becomes symbolic, poetic, archetypal. Perhaps this is what dreaming, and art, are for.

2015

PART FIVE

The Journey of the Stamp Animals

The Journey of the Stamp Animals

WHEN I was a small child in the 1940s, in a country town at the bottom of Australia, there existed in my life a book called *The Journey of the Stamp Animals*. It was the story of four Australian animals who somehow got off the stamps on which they were printed, and set out on a long and difficult pilgrimage—destination forgotten (by me).

Their travels were complicated by the fact that each animal was able to eat only things that were the same colour as the stylised stamp picture of itself that it had escaped from: the kangaroo could eat only yellow things, the sheep mauve, and so on. The roo could feast on butter, but the poor sheep had to keep searching for obscure things like wisteria, a plant I had not at that stage heard of.

The book's illustrations were most unsettling. I pored many times over a picture of the Foxy Roadhouse, a sort of nightclub where foxes went to dance. The four stamp animals, timid creatures with no experience of the world, had to creep past this wicked establishment, whose open doors let fall across the pavement a strip of smoky light. Inside the building, glamorous vixens in tiaras and plunging-necked cocktail gowns were gliding about in the arms of their tuxedoed, snarling partners; and all the foxes' clothes must have had special slits at the back, for out of their skirts and trousers gushed great, curved, furry tails. It was an image—sexual, sinister, intensely metropolitan—that thrilled me, as I lay on my bed in my sensible cotton pyjamas, in the humble town of Geelong beside its quiet bay.

But here's the really weird part. Except for members of my immediate family, no Australian I've mentioned the book to, in subsequent years, has had any knowledge of it whatsoever. I used to ask people about it all the time, but everyone looked blank. I started to think I must have dreamt it, or that it was a figment of my family's fantasy of itself.

Then ten years ago I wrote for *Vogue* magazine a little piece about childhood books, in which I mentioned the mysterious stamp animals and the deep effect they'd had on me. Soon the magazine forwarded to me a letter from an old woman living in a suburb of Sydney. Her daughter had spotted my article and brought her the cutting. Her name was Phyllis Hay. She was excited: she wanted me to know that she was the writer of the book.

It existed! A real Australian person had written it! We corresponded. I asked if she had a spare copy. She said she had only one left, but would lend it to me if I promised to return it. In due course it arrived. I hardly dared to open it. But when I did, out of its battered pages flowed in streams, uncorrupted, the same alarming joy it had brought me as a child, before everything in my life had happened. The wisteria was as mauve and as hard to reach, the stamp animals as sweet and determined, the foxes' tails as erotically forceful as I had remembered them. I gloried in the book and in the vindication of my memories. Regretfully, at last, I posted it back.

I heard from its author only once more. She wrote again to tell me that, on the strength of my recommendation, she had suggested to the publisher that they might reissue the book. She was sad to tell me that they had shown no interest at all.

Since then I've found that the library at Sydney University has a copy. I could take a bus and a train and another bus and go and read it—handle it, smell it, look at it—any time I liked. But I never do. I don't want *The Journey of the Stamp Animals* to exist anywhere except in the imaginations of its author and me. I don't know if she is still alive. I even manage to keep forgetting her name. Her book is one of those treasures of memory that I have to keep in its own little box, in case it leaks away.

2000

Worse Things than Writers Can Invent

Colonel Chabert, directed by Yves Angelo

February 8, 1807, somewhere in Prussia. Evening is falling over a smoky, littered battlefield. The sky is full of bloody clouds, the ground patchy with thin snow. A burial detail of soldiers in broad-skirted, belted overcoats, caked from waist to heel in mud, laboriously sorts through the casualties of a French cavalry regiment. The soldiers strip the stiffening corpses and haul them to mass graves.

Among the corpses lies the commander of the regiment, Colonel Chabert. A Russian split his skull with a tremendous sabre blow, and over his fallen body rode fifteen hundred horsemen in the famous charge which, on this day, decided the Battle of Eylau for Napoleon.

Ten years later, Chabert's death is a historical fact, described in *Victoires et Conquêtes*. So who is this bedraggled, dirty old vagabond (Gérard Depardieu) 'with his hat screwed on to his head', a figure of fun to clerks and messenger boys, who keeps doggedly presenting himself at the office of the ambitious young Paris lawyer Maître

Derville with his claim to be Colonel Chabert?

If he is Chabert, where has he been all these years? And what will his reappearance mean to Madame the erstwhile Comtesse Chabert, who, since she received official notification of his death in battle, has not only put the fortune he left her to such good use that within eighteen months of being widowed she was already worth 40,000 francs a year, but has remarried and had two children with her second husband, Comte Ferraud, a man eaten up with a fierce desire to be elevated to the peerage?

Comte Ferraud (André Dussollier) lives well on his wife's fortune, and she loves him—but because her money was amassed under the rule of the now disgraced and exiled Napoleon, she and her cash cut little ice with the new powerbrokers of the Restoration. In fact, Madame la Comtesse (Fanny Ardant) is so seriously tainted that Comte Ferraud is given a none-too-subtle hint, by a man he is trying to impress, that his political career would be sure to accelerate smartly were he to divorce the countess and marry one of the daughters of an ageing peer who might be counted on to pass his rank down to a suitably placed son-in-law.

While the count is being given this advice, his wife entertains guests in a drawing room to the elegant strains of a string quartet. In an alcove off the room, her husband pays court to a peer of the realm and his offsiders. The count presses on the peer not one fabulous cigar but two, three. 'He's bribing me!' jokes the peer suavely, taking the whole box. Then he offers his advice: 'You must *cut*. It should be surgical. An excision.' The breathless harshness of this scene is screwed tighter by the unfocused blob of white that floats in the background among the guests listening to the music: it's the countess's face, turning and turning towards the alcove, where she guesses her fate is being decided. One thing which would seal it to her eternal disadvantage is the return of her first husband.

This gloriously meaty movie is based on a minor story by Honoré de Balzac, king of nineteenth-century French realists. Its screenplay, by Jean Cosmos and director Yves Angelo, is a rarity in that it assumes adult intelligence in its audience. The dialogue dances and glances, packed tight with irony, menace, innuendo.

And the four main actors are up to it on every level. Angelo uses intense shots of faces: we see them working to hide, master, simulate emotions. The characters' movements are slow and deliberate, as if they were straining to force a path against the powerful currents of other people's desires, which are at least as obsessive as their own. To these people, as it was to Balzac, society is a seething, merciless swamp of competing ambitions.

Balzac was fascinated by lawyers, and Fabrice Luchini as Derville, the man so clever that he rarely sleeps and can concentrate on a dozen things at once, almost steals the show. His character is exquisitely worked. At times it verges on the comic, but our laughter is tinged with fear. He is small, very bright-eyed, a whisperer, a smiler, a percher on the extreme edge of sofas. There is something reptilian in the sheen of his alertness. 'Lawyers,' he remarks to Chabert, 'see worse things than writers can invent. Our offices are sewers that no one can clean.'

This is a story about different kinds of death, and about honour. The range of its sympathies is very broad. It is shocking and convincing on matters as various as the way aristocrats and the wealthy speak in front of their servants, and the brilliant, suicidal madness of a cavalry charge. It's a film that makes us work. It feeds the part of us that ordinary cinema sends home still howling with hunger.

1995

How to Marry Your Daughters

IT'S two centuries this year since Jane Austen's *Pride and Prejudice* was published. You'd need to have spent your life in a cave not to know about Mr Fitzwilliam Darcy, the ill-natured, land-owning über-spunk; Miss Elizabeth Bennet, sharp as a tack with a will of her own; her skewed array of sisters; her disengaged, ironic father; and her insufferable mother, the archetypal nineteenth-century airhead. They're part of the tissue of every literate person's mind.

But I confess that when I opened the novel last week and was greeted by its famous first sentence, which everybody, including me, claims to know by heart, I wasn't quite sure when, or even whether, I had read the book before. I sharpened a pencil and sat down at the kitchen table.

Austen blasts off with a fast-moving passage of dialogue between Mr and Mrs Bennet that lays out their relationship—her garrulous stupidity, his dry, self-protective 'teazing'—and the central matter of the tale: the business of getting their five daughters married. My God, Mrs Bennet is appalling. Every time her husband opens his mouth he takes revenge on her: today he is punishing her by means of a sadistic reticence about Mr Bingley, a wealthy, single young gentleman who has moved into their neighbourhood and set it abuzz.

The Bennets throw a dinner party for Bingley, who brings along his best friend, Mr Darcy. Handsome. Ten thousand a year. Large estate in Derbyshire. But wait. Darcy has a forbidding countenance. Elizabeth overhears him make a disobliging comment on her person and on the company. He's the most disagreeable man in the world, 'ate up with pride'. Everybody hopes that he will never come there again.

Nobody in this society (except the soldiers) has to do anything that would nowadays be thought of as work, though some of the less brilliant among them have made their money 'in trade', or 'in the north'. They drive about to parties and dances, or take tea in each other's pleasant dwellings, or go for long muddy walks.

For a while I kept expecting Austen to tell me what things looked like. Then I remembered that Joseph Conrad was exasperated by her novels: he couldn't *see* anything and it drove him crazy. I accepted that the appearance of things is not what she cares about, though Elizabeth's 'weary ancles and dirty stockings', and later an army camp with 'its tents stretched forth in beauteous uniformity of lines', gave me a furtive visual thrill.

Elizabeth and her adorable elder sister Jane, who is plainly going to wind up marrying Bingley, no matter what obstacles Austen might throw in their path, have cornered the brains, sweetness and decency of their family. Anyone who's ever read a book can see that Darcy will have to be brought to heel as much by the rules of narrative as by Elizabeth's admirable character and rigorous self-command.

Yet a source of chaos is needed to disrupt and delay the graceful blossoming of the plot. Austen has it covered. Younger sisters three and four, Lydia and Kitty, are 'vain, ignorant, idle and uncontrouled'. A militia regiment arrives in the neighbourhood. The place swarms with officers. A highly appealing fellow by the name of Wickham strolls on to the stage, eclipsing (even for Elizabeth) the snobbish Darcy.

I am no Janeite, but I knew Wickham's type. His charm is too rapid and shallow, too easy, for a heroine of Elizabeth's calibre. She falls for it, though, and takes at face value his tales of Darcy's treacherous dealings.

I lowered the blinds against the heat, unplugged the phone and moved operations to my *sopha*, where, dispos'd among charmingly group'd cushions, I settled in for the duration.

In order to keep my eye on how Austen was actually doing things, I was having to work hard against the seduction of her endlessly modulating, psychologically piercing narrative voice, her striding mastery of the free indirect mode.

'To interrupt a silence which might make him fancy her affected by what had passed...'

'Their indifference restored Elizabeth to the enjoyment of all her original dislike.'

'It was a wonderful instance of advice being given without being resented.'

So it came as a surprise to me that Mr Darcy makes Elizabeth his first proposal—which she repels in a scene of breathtaking muscle and spark—on page 210. Wasn't this rather premature? Had she hung out the flags of love too soon? I tilted the book and examined its profile. Exactly halfway! The cunning minx! She was going to make me wait another 218 pages for a resolution! Torn between despair and violent longing, I was obliged to rise from my sopha and take a turn around the drawing room.

Darcy, rejected and mortally offended, lurks in the garden. He emerges from behind a hedge and gives Elizabeth a letter, an elegantly written disclosure of Wickham's 'vicious propensities', his 'life of idleness and dissipation', and his corrupt behaviour towards Darcy's innocent younger sister. Elizabeth is thrown back upon herself in a most bracing manner.

Here Austen gives us five enthralling pages of *Elizabeth thinking*. She reasons like a lawyer, or rather, like a jury, weighing up evidence, assertion, argument. She turns on herself the cool, unsparing light of her moral intelligence, and finds herself wanting.

Yet Austen never lets us, or Elizabeth, off the hook of her own detached wit: 'Not a day went by without a solitary walk, in which she might indulge in all the delight of unpleasant recollections.' And in the sobering facts and reasoning that stream through this chapter, in which Elizabeth is forced to acknowledge to herself the ghastliness of her own family and the rightness of Darcy's dislike of them, I almost missed the pained and gentle last line of his farewell letter: 'I will only add, God bless you.'

Lydia Bennet, at sixteen, is a piece of trash. She earns our contempt not by eloping, but by jeering at a social inferior, an innocent waiter who has just served her: 'But he is such an ugly fellow! I never saw such a long chin in my life.'

We don't need Austen to explain how Lydia's coarse behaviour risks destroying her sisters' marriageability. A line of dominos will topple whispering to the ground if she is not reined in. And Austen does not scruple to sheet home Lydia's awfulness to her ill-matched parents. Instead of putting up a sturdy resistance to his wife's idiotic indulgence, Mr Bennet has retired to his study and his sarcasm, and left his younger daughters to their own devices.

In a letter of shattering selfishness that Lydia dashes off to her married friend, merrily telling her that she and Wickham have run away, she sends a message to a servant: 'I wish you would tell Sally to mend a great slit in my worked muslin gown.'

If the story had not by now become so dark, this joltingly sexual image would have made me laugh out loud. And what can mend the *great slit* that Lydia has torn in the story? While Darcy, using all his wealth and power behind the scenes, is picking up the pieces left by her heedless rampage, Austen will not allow Lydia to redeem herself. She pushes the girl's narcissism so far that it becomes grotesque, hilarious; yet I laughed with heart in mouth.

I writhed with joy on my sopha when Elizabeth takes it right up to Mr Darcy's aunt, the monstrous Lady de Bourgh, who intends her sickly daughter to marry Darcy. Under their parasols, in the copse, the two women go several savage rounds. The domineering old hag fails to lay a glove on our nimble, steely heroine.

But around page 387 I started to feel restless. All the loose ends were being tidied up and put away. It was a wrap. Wouldn't any ragged threads be left hanging, for me to be going on with?

And here she comes again, the relentless Lydia. Three pages before the end she writes the newly married Elizabeth a truly outrageous letter: 'I am sure Wickham would like a place at court very much…Any place would do, of about three or four hundred a year; but however, do not speak to Mr Darcy about it, if you had rather not. Your's, &c.'

I sprang off my sopha at last, strode to the freezer for a slug of Absolut, and raised my glass in silent respect. A toast to the Empress, Jane Austen. God bless Elizabeth Bennet and Mr Darcy, and the current of deep, warm erotic attraction that flows between them.

And long live the Lydias of this world, the slack molls who provide the grit in the engine of the marriage plot; for without them it would run so smoothly that the rest of us would fall into despair.

2013

X-ray of a Pianist at Work

Thirty-two Short Films about Glenn Gould

J. S. Bach is God, as far as I'm concerned, and the pianist Glenn Gould was one of his major prophets. Prophets, we know, come from the desert, but Gould—who died in 1982 aged only fifty— was a Canadian, and the desert that haunted him was 'the idea of north'—vast, unpopulated fields of snow. In the opening shot of this memorable work, a black speck appears on a white screen. As it moves towards us, growing legs, becoming a man tramping across snow, the soundtrack emerges tentatively out of silence: the whisper of a note, as if imagined, then a phrase, and then we are in the aria, meditative and slow, of Bach's *Goldberg Variations*.

This movie could narrowly be classed as documentary, but we're in 1994, and young Québécois director François Girard skips and slides nimbly among modes, using talking-head interviews, abstract animation, acted sequences he wrote himself, contemplations of the machinery of a grand piano, even an X-ray sequence of a pianist at work. The scope of the film has an attractive freedom, as if Girard were roving over a field of information and impression so rich that he could never exhaust it or his own ideas about it; but because the bottom line is always Bach's music, there is also in the film a satisfying sense of structure—that the thing is making sense, as it unfolds, on a level somewhere underneath your feet, so that you can trust it not to get lost in its constant changes, or wander away in whim.

Gould was a child prodigy. He became a cranky, nerdish, brilliant, verbose, pill-popping, hypochondriacal, introverted control freak, who conducted his most intimate relationships by telephone, and played the piano crouched on a specially doctored chair, contorting his body, uttering rapt murmuring hums, and fantastically conducting with whichever hand was free. He drove some critics and audiences insane, but many more to flights of joyous hyperbole. The friends he had were madly loyal to him, to the point of staying on the end of the phone, when he would call to rave in the middle of the night, till they fell asleep; children would find their father stretched out on the rug at first light, Gould's voice still rabbiting on in his oblivious ear.

At the peak of his fame as a concert performer he gave it up. He hated travel, feared planes; the life excruciated him, it made him sick. So he retired to the recording studio, where he could exercise a degree of control over his production of music which, when you first grasp its obsessiveness and daring, administers a sharp shock to any listener still clinging to a romantic ideal of performance as bounded by the limits of human ability in time.

I still remember the jolt I felt when a musician friend explained to me that Gould *recorded the two hands separately*. But—but—isn't that a swiz? Gould was blatant about this. He called it 'creative cheating' and it was an article of faith: you and the technology put yourselves at the service of the music. To him, his studio performance didn't end when he stood up from the instrument: it had barely begun. And this is why, when you listen to Gould's records, you never get the sense (as you do at times with just about any other keyboard player, however great, playing, say, one of Bach's massive fugues) that for a couple of seconds he's lost the map of the voices, that the thing has blurred into a forest without tracks. The perfectionism of the editing gives Gould's versions the gorgeous clarity, the three-dimensionality in which Bach's architecture is revealed.

Does this make Gould sound like only a brilliant machine? In one of this movie's thirty-two little hymns to the pianist, Girard cuts back and forth between a bunch of recording technicians in their lit booth, squabbling about whether black or white coffee is worse for you, and a darkened, cathedral-like space where Gould (played by actor Colm Feore) is listening to the playback of what he has just recorded. He is on his feet. His white shirt is bunched round his gawky torso, crushed and hanging out of his pants. His cuffs are unbuttoned and his sleeves are loose. His hair is on end. And he is dancing by himself in the dark, slowly, like a crazy angel in a white robe. His neck is on angles of ecstasy, his eyes are closed, his arms are high, his face melts in an expression of almost sexual transport. It's an image of bliss—and of the most intense solitude.

This movie is not meant to be biography. You can find out more facts about Gould by reading a book. What Girard has made is an original tribute to an extraordinary musician—and he has put the music first, even before the character. He has used the music as the film's defining formal principle. You will rush out of the cinema and straight to the nearest record shop, your nerves still zinging with the electric charge that Gould gets out of those fugues, those two- and three-part inventions—and later, when the adrenalin rush subsides, with the gratitude that comes after you have listened to him play this music.

1994

Gall and Barefaced Daring

I WAS well into my forties when I came upon Barbara Baynton's story 'The Chosen Vessel', and I have never got over it. It is shocking, and dreadful: a lone woman huddles with a tiny baby in an undefendable bush house at night, while a tramp armed with a knife slinks around it in the dark, seeking a way in. The terror Baynton evokes is elemental, sexual, unabashedly female in a way one hardly expects to read in literature of her time. Under the title 'The Tramp', the story appeared in the *Bulletin* in 1896. It was the first she ever published. She was thirty-nine.

A century later, I wrote an essay about a winter night I had spent alone in a shack on the edge of a forest. A male writer I showed it to was irritated by my anxious fantasies of marauding men, and by the mental manoeuvres I had had to perform in order to calm myself for sleep. I suppose he saw it as a piece of crude feminism. I have never got over this, either; and whenever I re-read 'The Chosen Vessel' I experience a deep solidarity with both its main character and its writer.

Baynton's best-known story is probably 'Squeaker's Mate'. Here the bush woman is stripped of every vestige of femininity. She is child-less, even 'barren' —a tough, skilled timber-getter who smokes a pipe and always carries 'the heavy end of the log'. Somehow this tireless worker has taken up with Squeaker, a bloke whom even the other men recognise as a whingeing bludger: to them, 'her tolerance was one of the mysteries'. A falling tree terribly wounds her. The story is an account of a power struggle between the feckless man and the silent, devastated woman whom he leaves to lie in a corner of their shack, attended only by her dog. Every time I read it I am astonished by Baynton's gall, the barefaced daring of the thing. It's driven by a contained, contemptuous rage that no woman of spirit can fail to recognise, or to share.

Baynton was born a decade before Henry Lawson, but by the time she began to publish he was already a famous writer. Determined as she was to write from deep within a woman's point of view, in her best work she can leave him sounding almost sentimental. Yes, Lawson's 'The Drover's Wife' is a great story. We fear for the hard-working, faithful, level-headed mother. We shed tears for her gutsy little son, for the brave dog, for the 'sickly daylight' that breaks over the bush. The story is what people nowadays call 'iconic'. We can safely admire it. We no longer even need to read it: everyone knows what it stands for.

But Baynton's bush wife inhabits a different universe. Weakened by her absent husband's cold mockery, she is not fighting for her family. No bushcraft, no weary stoicism can save her from sexual attack. She is lost out there in shrieking, existential abandonment. Her tale is never going to be an icon. It is too hair-raising, too hyster-ical—too close to women's craziest and most abject suffering.

Like any writer, she is not always at her best. Her sentences can strike the modern ear as clogged and heavy-handed, like Victorian interior decoration. You can feel her sometimes putting on side, striking writerly poses, indulging in misty poeticisms: *betimes*, she says, or *'twas a dingo*; *her heart smote her*, or *ever and ever she smiled*. Her desire to convey Australian speech leads her into passages of dialogue so manically phonetic that the only way to traverse them is to read them aloud, when they reveal her superb ear—but at what cost! I long to take the pencil to these extravaganzas, to drag her into my own century and hit her over the head with Elmore Leonard's dictum: 'If it sounds like writing, I rewrite it.'

But, my God, when she hits her straps she can lay down a muscular story.

> She drew out the saw, spat on her hands, and with the axe began weakening the inclining side of the tree.
>
> Long and steadily and in secret the worm had been busy in the heart. Suddenly the axe blade sank softly, the tree's wounded edges closed on it like a vice. There was a 'settling' quiver on its top branches, which the woman heard and understood. The man, encouraged by the sounds of the axe, had returned with an armful of sticks for the billy. He shouted gleefully, 'It's fallin', look out.'
>
> But she waited to free the axe.
>
> With a shivering groan the tree fell, and as she sprang aside, a thick worm-eaten branch snapped at a joint and silently she went down under it.
>
> ('Squeaker's Mate')

At their height, her dry, sinewy sentences stride forward powered by simple verbs. She knows how to break off at a breathless moment. She is familiar with labour, fear and abandonment. Her rendering of dogs and their meaning is very fine. She knows the landscape, with its bleak terrors and its occasional beauties. She has observed with a merciless eye the dull stupidity and squalor that poverty brings. She is not going to gussy it up.

Between Two Worlds, the enthralling biography of Baynton written by her great-granddaughter the late Penne Hackforth-Jones, makes it clear that the six stories in *Bush Studies*, the core of her small output, draw directly on the first half of her life.

She was born Barbara Lawrence in 1857, the seventh of eight children, at Scone in the Hunter Valley of New South Wales, where her immigrant father was a timber worker and coffin-maker. She seems to have been a strange, short-sighted, grittily emotional girl, a passionate reader of the few books she could get hold of, and possessed by confused fantasies of escape and adventure.

As a teenager she answered an advertisement for an up-country housekeeper. After a gruelling train trip to the property on the north-western plains of New South Wales, the naïve girl was coarsely challenged, humiliated and sent packing. A few years later, in her early twenties, with little more than her hard-won literacy and numeracy to recommend her, she was hired as a governess by the Fraters, a Scottish grazing family of impressive style but varying fortunes, whose glamorous son she soon married.

Set up by his disapproving father near Coonamble on the Castlereagh River, the handsome horseman Alex Frater soon showed his true colours. He drank, he gambled, he flirted with girls fresher and prettier than his clever, overworked, furious wife. The property slid into disarray while he went off droving and boozing for months at a time, leaving her and their babies without protection. The theme of a weakened and dependent person alone at night in a flimsy bush dwelling, which occurs again and again in Baynton's work, surely originates here.

By the time Frater had seduced and impregnated Barbara's

young niece Sarah, who had come to help her with the children, the iron had entered Barbara's soul. In 1889 she blasted her way out of the marriage, keeping custody of their three children. Her divorce, according to Hackforth-Jones, was 'the four-hundred-and-fifty-first of the colony'. Throughout her life Barbara liked to deliver a terse piece of advice to her daughter Penelope: 'If you make yourself a doormat, don't be surprised if you're walked on.'

Poor Sarah's fate enacted this bitter wisdom. She toiled on in wretched poverty, bearing more and more children to the ever-unreliable Frater, until soon after the birth of the ninth she fell into despair, and died in a Sydney mental hospital.

Meanwhile, Barbara shook the dust of the bush from her feet and lit out for Sydney. She was engaged as a housekeeper in pleasant Woollahra by the respected Dr Thomas Baynton, a widower more than twice her age. Barbara had learnt from her former mother-in-law how to conduct herself among educated people. Within a year, and the day after her divorce from Frater was finalised, she and the doctor were married.

Though only in her early thirties, she had experienced enough affront, desolation and rage to fuel a lifetime's literary output. Now, sharing an orderly urban life with a man she loved and respected, she could begin to write.

It irked her that some of her contemporaries were starting to romanticise, or to present in comic form, what she knew as the grinding slog and suffering of people who worked the land. She would make it her business to show the truth.

No one in Australia would publish *Bush Studies*, so she took it to London, where she met the usual insults dealt out to colonials; she even contemplated burning the manuscript and going home. But at last, in 1902, the book appeared in both London and Sydney. A. G. Stephens, who had first run her work in the *Bulletin*, opined ludicrously that the stories offered 'a perverse picture of our sunny, light-hearted, careless land'; but Baynton had many admiring reviews, and felt at last established.

Nothing else she published packs the raw punch of *Bush Studies*. Her natural form is the short story. Her novel *Human Toll* contains powerful and sensitive passages, but her obsession with phonetic dialogue is frustrating and fatiguing. One forgets her poetry with relief.

But what a woman! When her dear Dr Baynton died, she inherited and sensibly invested a comfortable fortune. In London during World War I she was a generous host to many a lost Australian serviceman on leave. She fought her way up the social ladder in the most audacious way. Her third husband was a baron who had converted to Islam. He was offered the vacant throne of Albania. To Barbara's great disappointment he refused it. The marriage lasted barely a year.

By now, though certain good friends never gave up on her, she seemed stuck in the role of the perverse dowager in jewels and long white gloves, known for her jealousy, bursts of wild rage and equally violent remorse. She returned to Melbourne and took up residence next door to her daughter, whose husband had the sense of humour and strength of character to keep the matriarch in line. Her grandchildren she thrilled by writing and reading aloud to them cautionary tales 'of human unpleasantness and folly'. These stories were never published, and when at the age of seventy-two the champagne-drinking old termagant died, her faithful daughter, who loved her, threw them into the fire.

2012

The Rules of Engagement

United 93

On a lovely autumn morning in early September 2001, United Airlines Flight 93 took off from Newark, bound for San Francisco. Among its passengers were four young Islamic hijackers, armed with knives and explosives. While flight 93 was in the air, three other hijacked planes hit the World Trade Center and the Pentagon. By 10.03 that morning, flight 93 had missed its hijackers' target, the Capitol in Washington, and slammed into a field near Shanksville, Pennsylvania. No one survived.

Five years have passed. We have tried to absorb the facts and find the meanings of that day. We've had to make peace with them, in our private ways, because we've got to keep on living in what is known as the post-9/11 world. So how can we bear, now, to be dragged through it again, to sit in the dark for two hours and watch the story's relentless deathward plummet, in what feels hideously like real time?

Two things make it possible. First, the exemplary tonal and

technical brilliance of *United 93* as a piece of filmmaking; and second, the fact that some of the passengers on flight 93, knowing that nothing could save them, found the nerve to plan and launch a wild, last-ditch attack on the hijackers. The laws of feature-film narrative are ironclad. Without this burst of hopeless defiance, we would have no curve, no plot, no movie.

United 93's director, Paul Greengrass (*Bloody Sunday*, *The Bourne Supremacy*), is British. Perhaps this is why he has been able to steer clear of the heroic posturing and sentimental appeals to patriotism we might have feared in a native version of the story.

At the same time, the physical world in which *United 93* unfolds is effortlessly American. Greengrass has cast a mixture of obscure actors and actual airline workers and flight-control personnel. Part of his remarkable achievement is to establish, in layer after relaxed layer, the texture of an ordinary working morning—to make the casual, the mundane glow under the shadow of its annihilation.

First, though, in the opening shots we see the hijackers at prayer in their cheap motel. Fresh sunlight streams past its windows. Their faces are sombre, and very young. The camera averts its gaze, accords them privacy as they wash and shave their faces, limbs and genitals. They slide knives into their belts. Then, as they step out of their cab at Newark and join the check-in queue, their approach to the plane is intercut with cheerful footage of what they have come to destroy.

The flight crew ambles with its wheelie suitcases down the pristine aisles of the aircraft. Outside, mechanics in overalls stand under the plane's belly, gazing up at the curved metal. The camera roams along the rows of passengers as they gather at the gate lounge, engaged in the benign trivia of the departing. One of the hijackers, his face rigid, calls a number on his mobile: '*Ich liebe dich*,' he murmurs, unanswered, as if to a machine, '*Ich liebe dich*.' Among the readers and talkers and eaters, a grandmother sits quietly working at her crochet, a pastime that, along with knitting, has vanished from planes since that day. The plainer the people—coarse skin, double chins, unglamorous clothes—the more their tiny preparatory actions strain our nerves.

Before flight 93 has even got the signal to taxi, we cut to the command centre of the Federal Aviation Administration, where workers at their screens call out in bewilderment as one plane in flight, then another, drops off the radar or suddenly changes course. 'They think they got a hijack!' 'This is sim?' 'No! Real world! I heard it in my ear! Check it out!' At Newark, ignorant flight 93 turns on to the sunny runway and thunders towards take-off.

The deluge of information that Greengrass has to handle defies précis. We get swamped by it, just as the air traffic people do. In dim command centres and control towers, people in headphones stand gaping before TV screens. Smoke gushes from the World Trade Center. The second plane plunges voluptuously into the glistening wall of steel and glass. The camera itself becomes panicky, incredulous, mimicking our shock.

But Greengrass drives the narrative on with a furious authority, leaping back and forth between the dawning horror on the ground and the pale, peaceful innocence of flight 93, where the pilots are being served their little breakfasts on plastic trays, and a lady politely asks the attendant for a glass of water to take her pills.

And then the first hijacker, shouting in praise of Allah, throws himself on a passenger and stabs him to death in a welter of blood. The others murder the pilots and haul their bodies out of the cockpit. The austere, devout young man in glasses ('*Ich liebe dich*') is now in command of the plane. While his panting comrade sluices blood off his hands with a bottle of spring water, the new pilot wedges a colour photo of the Capitol among the controls and turns the aircraft towards Washington.

This is not a film about heroes. It's not even, thank God, about characters: we don't 'get to know' anyone. It's a vast ensemble piece on speed, a densely textured, brilliantly edited, unerringly paced creation of chaos and horror.

On the ground, the civilians shout for the military, and the military begs in vain for orders. The chain of command is non-existent. The fighters they get into the air are not armed. 'Can we engage? Do we have any communication with the President at all? How about the Vice-President? Holy shit! What the fuck? What are the rules of engagement?' The only person with the nous to take charge is the guy who's been promoted the day before to national operations manager at the Federal Aviation Administration. He cuts through the uproar. 'Everyone lands,' he says, 'regardless of destination.'

'You're gonna shut down the entire country?' cries his deputy. 'Take a minute!'

'Shut down the airspace! We're at war! With someone!'

Flight 93, awash with blood, goes screaming across the bright morning sky. In the cockpit the hijackers hear radio reports of the twin towers and Pentagon strikes: 'The brothers have hit both targets!' Some passengers pray and weep, hunch over borrowed mobiles to whisper farewells, sob out promises to their children, make declarations of love.

But others, hiding from the hijackers among the high seat-backs, start to rage and mutter. It takes one cool head to galvanise them. 'No one's going to help us,' he says. 'We've got to do it ourselves.' An ex-pilot thinks he can fly the plane, if they can break down the door. A bunch of them seize whatever weapons they can find—forks, a fire extinguisher—and rush the hijackers, battering the cockpit door with a heavy steel trolley.

Their violence sends a charge of crazed energy through the film's last minutes. The air is thick with howls of terror and anguish, with cries to God in Arabic. The camera, too, is in there fighting: things blur and lurch, something splits apart, wires are trailing. The cockpit's windscreen fills with city streets, then with the fresh dark-green grass-blades of a meadow.

I have a rule of thumb for judging the value of a piece of art. Does it give me energy, or take energy away? When I staggered out of *United 93* this rule had lost traction. I realised I had spent most of the screening crouching forward with my hand clamped around my jaw. Something in me had been violently shifted off-centre. Outside in the street there seemed to be a dark grey cloud over everything. An excruciating pity for all material things overwhelmed me. This flayed sensation lasted about two days, then gradually dissipated. Then I was left with a confused mixture of respect for the craft of the movie, amazed admiration for the people who charged the hijackers, and the same old haunting question: why do stories matter so terribly to us, that we will offer ourselves up to, and later be grateful for, an experience that we know is going to fill us with grief and despair?

2006

The Rapture of Firsthand Encounters

THE great American journalist Janet Malcolm will turn eighty next year. This fact has hit me amidships. She is the writer who has influenced and taught me more than any other. I have never met her, or heard her speak, but I would know her written voice anywhere. It is a literary voice, composed and dry, articulate and free-striding, drawing on deep learning yet plain in its address, and above all fearless, though she cannot possibly be without fear, since she understands it so well in others.

The whole drive of her work is expressed, I think, in a phrase she uses in one of the essays collected in *Forty-one False Starts*: 'the rapture of firsthand encounters with another's lived experience'.

Rapture is not too strong a word for the experience of reading Malcolm. You can feast on these essays, as on all her work. Nothing in them is slick or shallow. Her work is always challenging, intellectually and morally complex, but it never hangs heavy. It is airy, racy, and mercilessly cut back, so that it surges along with what one critic has called 'breathtaking rhetorical velocity'. It sparkles with deft character sketches. It bounds back and forth between straight-ahead reportage and subtle readings of documents and diaries, of photographs and paintings.

Malcolm's way of perceiving the world is deeply dyed by the psychoanalytical view of reality. She never theorises or uses jargon. She simply proceeds on the assumption that (as she puts it in another book, *The Purloined Clinic*) 'life is lived on two levels of thought and act: one in our awareness and the other only inferable, from dreams, slips of the tongue, and inexplicable behaviour'. This approach, coupled with her natural flair for metaphor and imagery, allows her almost poetic access to meaning in the way people dress and move, speak or decline to speak—and in her most famous and disputed concern, trust and betrayal in the relations between journalists and their subjects.

You feel the intense pleasure she gets from thinking. She keeps coming at things from the most unexpected angles, undercutting the certainty she has just reasoned you into accepting, and dropping you through the floor into a realm of fruitful astonishment, and sometimes laughter.

She skates past the traditional teachings on split infinitives or the undesirability of adjectives: like Christina Stead she will string adjectives and adverbs together in sinewy strands—half-a-dozen of them, each one working hard. An art magazine, she says, has 'an impudent, aggressively unbuttoned, improvised, yet oddly poised air'.

Her description of clothes and their meaning is deadly: 'a tall, thin, bearded man wearing tight jeans and high-heeled clogs'. Her brisk shorthand often has a sting in its tail: 'Wilson, who had an unhappy childhood in a mansion'; 'the look of a place inhabited by a man who no longer lives with a woman'. A young art critic speaks, she says, 'with the accent of that non-existent aristocratic European country from which so many bookish New York boys have emigrated'.

The longest piece in this collection, 'A Girl of the Zeitgeist', is a study of the New York art scene of the 1980s. Nothing could interest me less, I thought; but within a few sentences I found myself drawn into a scintillating anthropological investigation that I read greedily, realising that like any other microcosm this one could be studied with both entertainment and profit, and with a thrilling degree of enlightenment about the human project.

For Malcolm, life is unruly. She is gripped by artists' struggles to get command of it, not to be abject before it. But she pulls no punches. She will observe a person and the decor of his apartment, his shoes, his clothes, his way of cooking; she will switch on her reel-to-reel, start him talking, then stand back. Her ear is so finely tuned to speech, and her nerves to the unspoken, that later, when she sits at her desk, she will recreate her subject's utterances with a lethal accuracy, unfolding his character and world view like a fan.

She maintains a perfectly judged distance between her eye and its target. She does not suck up to the people she interviews, or try to make them like her by revealing her own personal life in exchange for their confidences. Her boredom threshold is high. She gives her subjects rope. She allows herself to be charmed, at least until the subject reveals his vacuity or his phoniness, and then she snaps shut in a burst of impatience, and veers away. Although at times she draws back in distaste, or contempt, or even pity, she is not someone who deplores the way of the world or desires to change it. She merely observes it with a matchless eye. In her work there is a complete absence of hot air.

She will not be read lazily. She assumes intelligence and expects you to work, to pace along with her. Her writing turns you into a better reader. There is no temptation to skim: its texture is too rich, too worldly, too surprising. She is brilliant at revealing things in stages, so you gasp, and gasp, and gasp again. She yokes the familiar with the strange in the way that dreams do—suddenly a wall cracks open and a flood of light pours in, or perhaps a perfectly aimed, needle-like beam. Reading her is an austerely enchanting kind of *fun*.

In the closing piece of *Forty-one False Starts*, fragments from 'an abandoned autobiography', Malcolm describes herself as 'someone who probably became a journalist precisely because she didn't want to find herself alone in the room'. What are those words *probably* and *precisely* doing there, bouncing off each other, striking a little chord of uncertainty? I dare to feel a rush of comradeliness. Ms Malcolm, Janet, we cannot do without you. Live in good health and keep writing, for at least another ten years. Dear boss, shine on.

2013

Hit Me

ONE morning I walked into the kitchen and found my son-in-law standing frozen in front of the TV. On the screen a bloke in a blue singlet was manhandling an electric guitar. I had never before witnessed such a noxious exhalation of inauthenticity.

'Who's *that*?'

'It's Russell Crowe. And his band, 30 Odd Foot of Grunts.'

There seems no end to the cataract of copy set off by Russell Crowe's movements through the world. His name is a byword for gracelessness and self-importance. The sight of him stepping out of a building, granite-faced in aviator glasses, can reduce the onlooker to helpless laughter. He and Nicole Kidman are the twin peaks of antipodean self-creation in the Hollywood of our time. One can no longer go out in public without having an opinion about him.

What was mine? First I challenged myself to write down everything I could remember about the films I had seen him in over the past fourteen years. Free-associating; no faking. As always in such tests of memory, the results were sparse.

Proof. Minor violence. Genevieve Picot sulking in a droopy cardigan. A camera? Hugo Weaving? No memory of Crowe.

Romper Stomper. Violence. Crowe fucking a girl, driving her up the bed with such force that her neck is bent against the wall.

LA Confidential. Violence. Detectives. Crowe asking Kim Basinger: 'Why me?' Crowe slumped in the back seat of Basinger's car, broken-boned and bandaged.

Spotswood. No violence. Worker asks boss to put drops in his eyes. Kick to kick in factory yard. No memory of Crowe.

The Sum of Us. No violence. Crowe as a gay tradesman. Jack Thompson laughing very loudly.

A Beautiful Mind. Crowe as a mathematical genius. Ivy. Mental illness. Codes. Think I cried. Felt worked over, irritated.

Master and Commander. Water. Sky. Naval battles. Crowe as captain. Sea burials. A fiddle, Crowe playing it. Men, boys. No women. Amputation. *Origin of Species*?

Gladiator. Missed it. Just lazy, nothing to do with Crowe. Annoyed at myself. Pasted into my diary a still of Crowe with huge glistening muscles and an undershirt of celestial blue.

The Insider. Missed it. Don't know why.

That was about the size of it. 'And wasn't there an Australian movie called *The Crossing*, way back?' said my daughter. 'Russell Crowe stood out. I thought, he's got something.'

So I loaded up at the video shop, shut myself into the house and drew the blinds for a week. Outside the window each day my son-in-law was digging and laying out our new vegetable patch, with his eighteen-month-old son strapped to his back. Whenever I took a break I could hear them out there in the sun, singing and making silly noises and laughing quietly. I was embarrassed by the sounds of warped manliness I imagined reaching them from my closed-in room: the shatter of gunfire, the growling of wild beasts, the screams of the dismembered, the oafish grunts and curses of skinheads, the occasional staccato outbreak of foul speech. There was something perverse about it, on a clean spring morning.

George Ogilvie's *The Crossing* takes place on Anzac Day in a country town. Bugles at dawn, Crowe and girlfriend asleep in a hayshed after making love, interiors smoky with golden light. Crowe's widowed mother is a clingy, sentimental drunk. How can he be a man? A nature boy, he's got the sweat sheen, the muscles, the scowl; he juts his jaw and fires guns into the air and poses wide-legged against a fierce blue sky; but he says 'chahnce' and wears tight white jeans, even when hunched under the open bonnet of a ute. Fast forward—but wait. Who's that playing his girlfriend? Woh! It's Danielle Spencer, the woman who's now his wife.

The most interesting thing about her, here, is that *she looks like him*. The broad forehead, the eyebrows in a permanent inverted V of earnestness. The meaty nose. The rare smile. Impertinent psychologising possessed me while the film redeemed itself with a splendidly Shakespearean car and train smash.

Proof, written and directed by Jocelyn Moorhouse, whose screenplay based on the novel *Eucalyptus* Crowe would years later allegedly feel competent to rewrite, is unusually inward and intense for an Australian movie—a triangle of emotional distortion and manipulation. Crowe plays a young kitchenhand in a restaurant with red-checked tablecloths. On the video case his eyes are a startling, innocent blue, something I haven't noticed on screen.

He, of course, is the Eros figure of the piece—the untutored bogan who brings a blast of freshness into the lives of a nasty Camberwell pair, a blind man played by Hugo Weaving and his spiteful housekeeper Genevieve Picot. Crowe, as a physical worker, is again covered in a sheen of sweat. While Weaving lectures him on aesthetics he gazes up intently, showing us big features, juicily indented lips, a dimpled chin, an interesting breadth of brow. There is a little quality here, some nameless thing. '*Everybody* lies!' he says to the neurotic Weaving, who suspects and thus meets betrayal everywhere; 'but not all the time, and that's the point!' In Crowe's roguish company Weaving laughs for the first time, an unnervingly jerky, nasal sound.

What the hell was Crowe doing in Mark Joffe's *Spotswood*, that same year? Gee, it was a sweet movie—hopelessly old-fashioned but warm and funny. Anthony Hopkins as the time-and-motion man politely subdues his greatness, but for the first time I feel that Crowe, as the salesman, is biding his time. Technically one can't fault him, but he's not engaged. He's already somewhere else.

My daughter found a letter I'd written her in 1992 after seeing Geoffrey Wright's *Romper Stomper*. Seems I liked it. 'Russell Crowe was the leader of the skins, the one who'd read *Mein Kampf* etc. He sounded more like a Scotch College boy than a psychopath—rounded vowels, strong inner self.' I wrote disdainfully of David Stratton's refusal even to see the movie. But now, at second viewing, I couldn't believe how much screen time is taken up with crane shots of boys running wildly in single file down narrow Footscray lanes. The brawl scenes too are interminable, adolescently gloried-in: later I noticed that the credits named five nurses. I started to fidget in my seat.

Crowe looms over the tale, unmodulated, with face of stone. He gets expression by jerking his jaw, swinging it from side to side. There's a fabulous final scene on a beach. Crowe does a grand death, twitching and spewing blood, and he leaves a pretty corpse, but the standout in *Romper Stomper* is mad-faced Daniel Pollock, who in real life died not long after. What a loss Pollock is: that delicacy, a puzzled complexity just starting to grow.

I hunted out my 1994 review of *The Sum of Us*, directed by Kevin Dowling and Geoff Burton. Crowe plays Jeff, a gay plumber. The blue singlet? A mullet? How hard it is, now, to imagine this: 'Jeff, a sweet-natured hulking boy whose self-esteem has taken a knock from a recent broken heart, comes home from the pub late on Friday night with a young gardener in tow.' Should I scour the video shops? But 'after a tantalising dip into a darker complexity it bounces straight back up to the surface and becomes what its provenance fates it to be—a sentimental exercise about love and family loyalty.' Okay, pass, though a small warmth lingers.

Here I skipped forward to 1997, Curtis Hanson's *LA Confidential*. Twenty minutes in and Crowe, as Officer Bud White, has beaten up a couple of creeps, torn the Christmas decorations off the house-front of a wife-bashing parole violator, and pressed money into the grateful victim's hand. Though I'm interested in detectives, I eschew them on screen; but *LA Confidential*, humming with the highly worked and disciplined craziness of the James Ellroy novel it's based on, is something else.

For a start it's beautiful. Every shot, every juxtaposition makes you gasp. The long, pale cars. The cream and white interiors of Kim Basinger's apartment, her private bedroom all sunny and embroidered. Hanson cuts away from Crowe (in a singlet) beating the shit out of a perp in a blind-dimmed room to an exterior shot of a sunlit skyscraper which is so blatantly, glowingly phallic that it's almost comical.

And the talent! It overflows. Guy Pearce as the idealistic prig, that porcelain face he's got, the vulnerable rimless glasses; Kevin Spacey as the celebrity crime stopper, his level, insolent, flat-eyed stare. Crowe, the violent crusader with the wounded soul, is at ease in this league. He has earned his place in these superbly lit montages of expressionless men in suits, painterly group shots of casual beauty, with a thick soundtrack of shifting feet and murmuring voices and, somewhere out of shot, a man sobbing.

For disgraced Officer Bud White in *LA Confidential* I am

prepared to forgive 30 Odd Foot of Grunts. I will even overlook the documented existence of a song called 'Swallow My Gift'. Go, Russ, go! Let Kim Basinger drive you to Arizona, and learn to be happy.

Now we come to the problem of Ron Howard's *A Beautiful Mind*. Why am I so reluctant to see it again? I don't know, but my resistance is adamantine. I try hard to remember what bugged me about it. I don't much like biopics. There's a scenery-chewing element to movies about 'the triumph of the human spirit' that I can't hack. Also, my week with Russell is running out and I've still got to plough through *Master and Commander*, *The Insider* and *Gladiator*. This isn't supposed to be encyclopaedic. If it were I'd have had to go back to *Neighbours*.

Life is short. Pass. And I'm only pretending to be sorry.

You can't talk about an actor's *oeuvre*. Directors have *oeuvres*. Actors have jobs. They have skills, they have luck, they have reputations, they have things they are known for doing well—and they risk getting stuck in their own groove. What Crowe does best is a certain sort of maleness: he is really good at violence, and at only just managing to hold back from violence. The thin veneer of his character's self-command is what makes him exciting to watch, if you like that sort of thing—and a woman can get pretty sick of the bloodletting that seems inseparable from Hollywood's narrow concepts of manliness.

Peter Weir's *Master and Commander*, concerning as it does the adventures of men and boys in the early nineteenth-century navy, turns on male codes and encompasses a great deal of violence, but in its flexible ideas of what manliness might be it displays a genial maturity. Its screenplay, issuing from a series of highly literate novels, holds firm, against the horrid brutality of a naval life, the formal starch of what is still eighteenth-century speech. Fourteen minutes in, the decks are running with blood and the ship is holed and wallowing, but 'If you please', they say, or 'May I beg you?' A tiny midshipman comforts the ship's doctor with the gift of a beetle. At table, officers burst into melodious song. The idea that a man might be an intellectual without losing face is given full worth.

Crowe as Captain Aubrey is a new proposition altogether. He's carrying a bit of weight—you could almost say embonpoint. The long hair in its queue and the newly rounded face suit him, as does the flattering three-cornered hat. And what are these smiles? These flashes of benevolence and good humour? I had got past my hostility to Crowe, I had even begun to admire him; but this was the first time I'd liked him. When he picked up his fiddle and sat down to play a duet with the doctor, I waited for a shudder of embarrassment to spoil it for me. It didn't come. I sat there in front of the TV thinking: He's even made me *believe in the violin*. I pressed pause, ran to the cupboard, and poured myself a glass of port.

What could one drink to make Ridley Scott's *Gladiator* bearable? Unable despite my best efforts to suspend disbelief, I was tormented by carping thoughts. Did they really have cafés in those Roman colonnades? How did Maximus keep his hair always at the perfect length, and who twirled those little kiss curls across his brow?

I enjoyed the Nuremberg-style extravaganzas. I was thrilled by the movie's gorgeousness, its subtle colours, the extraordinary palette of blues. When they carried Maximus's body away a fat tear plopped into my packet of bullets. But as soon as anyone spoke I had to get up and do some deep breathing. Those creaking rhetorical flourishes! 'You shall watch as I bathe in their blood.' 'The time for half-measures is over, Senator.' 'It takes a Nemperor to rule a Nempire.' 'It vexes me. I'm terribly *vexed*.' Coming to *Gladiator* as I did five years too late, I felt like Joaquin Phoenix's Commodus, all perfumed and fresh and *maquillé*, galloping up to his father Marcus Aurelius moments after the great greasy blackened brutes of Germania's army have been routed by the Romans at untellable expense of life and limb.

'Have I missed it?' lisps Commodus, springing out of his chariot. 'Have I missed the battle?'

His father regards him wryly. 'You've missed the war.'

The Insider I saved for last. I had managed since 1999 to avoid knowing the first thing about it. I didn't even know that Al Pacino, at whose shrine I have worshipped since *The Godfather II*, was in it. Again Crowe's character is struggling for honour in the world of men. This time he plays a man of science, Dr Jeffrey Wigand, a researcher for a giant tobacco company who is threatened with litigation if he breaks a confidentiality agreement about the harmful properties of their products.

'Tobacco's a sales culture,' says Pacino, as the tough *60 Minutes* producer who wants Wigand to spit the dummy on TV. 'Why'd you work for them?'

'They paid me a lot o' money.'

Treated with outrageous insolence by the company executives, Wigand begins to seethe with the desire to break his promise, cleanse himself of his compromises, and wreak revenge. But his only way of doing this is to put himself at the mercy of the commercial TV network CBS. Even a battle-hardened journalist like Pacino's Lowell Bergman, with his dark-circled eyes and husky voice, can't predict or control the treachery of his employers.

Can this blundering naïf, this tormented whistleblower, be Russell Crowe? He is unrecognisable, leached of vanity and self-regard. By holding his persona in check, he quadruples his power. His body, in the flapping suit, has grown all massive and square. Although his hair is grey, his eyes behind the unfashionable glasses are those of an unhappy, nerdish boy. His mouth is jammed hard in a straight line. His neck is rigid with suppressed emotion.

And the deep texture of the film! The camera always sliding at things from a surprising angle! The music—that countertenor soaring while Crowe, off his head with anger, belts a thousand white golf balls all over the driving range! What's going on here? My notebook and pencil slide to the floor.

The tobacco company finds a way to gag Wigand in Kentucky: he is threatened with prison if he speaks in court. The cynical brutality he's up against paralyses him, thickens the movie's air. Crowe's face is big, stunned, wounded, like a peasant's. 'How does one go to jail?' he asks the journalist. Outside the courthouse, watched by the hawkish Pacino, he paces on green grass. His loneliness is appalling. Cars pass in silence. All sound is suspended, except a mandolin strumming soft and fast. Nothing breathes. Then he speaks: 'Fuck it. Let's go to court.' The soundtrack explodes back into reality. That's when I started howling, and hardly stopped till the credits rolled. It's a splendid movie, grand and serious, and Crowe is the aching centre of it.

What has he gone through, what has he put others through, to get to this eminence? I roamed around the internet and found an interview with the director of *The Insider*, Michael Mann. 'How did you work with Crowe?' they ask him. Mann dodges it. 'I don't talk about some of that. Some of this stuff, it's just not right to be public about.'

I felt frustrated and abashed, as if I'd been caught snooping. When I told a friend I was writing a piece about Crowe, he fired up: 'Where do you get off? You've never met him, have you?' 'I'm only writing about his movies,' I said, miffed, and that's what I set out to do. But Crowe's public persona, noisy and humourless and strutting, is forever making rude gestures in the corner of my eye, demanding attention and cursing those who give it. The only way to block it out is to turn to his work, to watch with joy as he steps away into that free place where art happens.

2005

PART SIX

In the Wings

My First Baby

THIS isn't really a story. I'm just telling you what happened one summer when I was young. It was 1961, my first year away from home. I lived at Melbourne University, in a women's college on a beautiful elm-lined boulevard. I was free and happy. Everyone was clever and so was I.

When summer came and exams were over, I went home to Geelong. I could have hung around the house all day with my sisters and my brother. I could have gone swimming or read books. But I was a student now, and students had jobs. I typed on my little Hermes portable a neat letter of application to Bright and Hitchcocks, Geelong's biggest department store. They hired me for the Christmas rush. I could hardly wait to start.

They sent me to the basement. I went down a staircase with brass banisters, through the gardening and camping section, and into a stuffy dead-end corner. I had imagined books or cosmetics or nice cotton underwear, but I was to sell toys.

I liked it down there. The toys in those days were made of wood and paper and metal and cloth. We wrapped each purchase in a sheet of thick brown paper, and tied the parcel with string from a heavy ball that hung above the register. There wasn't time for scissors: you ran the string around your forefinger in a special loop and snapped it back against itself. I wore a white blouse and a big gathered cotton skirt with stiff petticoats, pulled in at the waist by a brown dog-collar belt. And stockings attached to a suspender belt, and shoes called 'flatties' which gave no support. My feet ached that summer. They ached rhythmically, like string quartets of pain, and, by the end of each day, like a great screaming Wagnerian orchestra.

But this is about another kind of pain.

On a certain shelf in our department stood the dolls. The goggle-eyed, sissy ones bored me. I despised their stiff hair and aprons, their tiny white shoes, their pink and useless feet. I sold a lot of them. I worked scornfully, packing and wrapping the ridiculous things in their cellophane-fronted boxes. I fancied myself an intellectual when aunts and mothers tilted their permed heads this way and that and smiled and went, 'Aaaaaah!'

But there was one doll that I did like. It lay flat on its back in a cardboard box. It was naked but for a nappy. Its torso was soft, its head was heavy. When you picked it up, its eyelids slid shut, its limbs flopped loosely and its head dropped back, exactly like a real baby. You had to hold it properly.

I came to feel that the doll was private and personal to me. I thought of buying it, but it was very expensive—and imagine an intellectual turning up at home with a doll. I didn't want anyone else to buy it. Nobody showed any lasting interest in it, but I kept stowing it behind other items, just in case. Every afternoon at 5.30, before I went home, I made sure the doll was still safe, at the back of the shelf.

The Christmas rush became intense. We sweated down there in our stuffy department. I had less and less time for the doll. Entire days would pass when I didn't go looking for it. Then one afternoon I saw a middle-aged woman lurking behind the shelf where it was kept. She stayed there for a suspiciously long time. In a lull, I slid over to see what she was up to.

She had dug the doll out of its box, and she was holding it in her arms. Her head was bent over it. She didn't even notice I was there. I couldn't see her face but there was something about her posture that made me pause. Even with her back to me, she was radiating 'keep off'.

I returned to the cash register. She stayed behind the shelf for ten minutes, fifteen minutes. I was seething with jealousy. She didn't bring anything to the counter. After a while, she emerged from behind the shelf and disappeared up the stairs. Every day at the same time, she came back. She never looked at us or spoke to us. She made a beeline through the crowd of Christmas shoppers to the shelf where the doll was kept, took it out of the box, and held it in her arms. If any of us had to pass her, she turned her face away. She had a limp perm and her clothes were drab. I looked at her hand, but I can't remember now whether she was wearing a ring.

I was nineteen and I thought of her as old. She had no right to be cuddling a doll. It was indecent. It mortified and enraged me. But once as I passed, in my jealousy, she glanced up and our eyes met. She held my gaze for a moment, with my doll in her arms, and flashed me a tiny, embarrassed smile. Her face was tired. It was absolutely ordinary. And into my head shot the thought: her real baby died, years ago, and she will never get over it.

I walked quickly past. Soon she put the doll down and drifted away up the stairs.

I don't remember what happened to the doll. Within three years I'd had two abortions, and within eight years, a child. The abortions I went into briskly, without conscious regret. But now I'm in my fifties, they've come back to haunt me. I've had to grieve for them, and mourn them. I never expected this to happen. It was awful, and it took a long time. When it first surged up in me, I remembered the woman in the toy department, and the look she gave me. For the first time I understood it, and I grieved for her as well.

2000

Big Brass Bed

EVERYONE was upset when the café changed hands. For years it had stood reticently on our main street. In winter a wood stove warmed it. Herbs grew in tubs along the path to the toilet. The quiet souls who ran it supplied toys and colouring books, and fresh copies of the *Guardian Weekly* and the *Financial Review* as well as the essential celebrity trash. They knew our names and were patient, pad in hand, with children's struggles to read the menu for themselves. They baked and served the most sensational savoury muffins. And their coffee was always perfect. On the last day nobody wanted to leave. Some of us cried.

The day the sheets of newspaper came down off the windows, I went in. The new young guy behind the counter had a shaved head and a Pearl Jam T-shirt. Not only did he give me one of those blank looks that are reserved for invisible women of my age, but he addressed me as 'sweetie'.

They were going for a '70s look: a lot of nauseous burnt orange; wood-framed paintings of sailing ships. The waiter brought me my latte in a glass shaped like a teacup. The head on it was thick and the right colour, but I looked at it resentfully.

Somebody else had got the *Age* first so I had to pay attention to the music. It was some band I'd never heard before, loud and boring. Making a mental note never to come here again, I took the first sip of coffee.

It was good. It was really quite excellent. I felt it go zinging smoothly along my veins, opening out my thoughts into a series of promising gateways. I would have to admit it was a perfect coffee. There was nothing I needed to write, but I was in the mood, so I got out my notebook and pencil, and looked around for something to describe.

The customer who'd bagged the *Age* was an oldish woman, a stranger, sitting opposite my table with her back to the wall. She looked ordinary and dull, like somebody's wife, or widow, or mother, or auntie, or nanna. Her hair was short and dyed, and she was wearing a loose linen shirt over pants cropped above the ankle. She was carrying some weight, and her feet were veiny, in their sensible, thick-soled sandals. She had a pencil in her hand and was doing the crossword. Her face was closed and crabby-looking.

Just as I was making a note of this, the music stopped, and a new CD began. A harmonica, thin and tentative. A young-sounding band, warm and modest and not yet famous, loped out of a faraway country. A nasal voice, quivering with melancholy, singing about a pick-up, about driving it down to LA. I sat up. Along with the caffeine, a stream of happy memory flowed through me, from thirty-five years ago.

The oldish woman at the other table kept her head down over the puzzle, but her lips were moving. I thought she was spelling out the clues, but then I saw the pattern: she was singing along. I stared at her, thunderstruck. We must be the same age.

And she kept going. She knew all the verses. Pictures on the wall. A big brass bed.

The waiter who had called me 'sweetie' dashed past my table. I called out: 'Hey. Who's the Neil Young buff?' He gave me a big, open grin as he hurried by: 'Oh, round here we've got a *thing* about him.'

I laughed. The woman doing the crossword raised her head and shot me a private smile. Her face was warm and open and pretty. She looked ten years younger. Before I could respond, she dropped her eyes again and went on working away with her pencil.

So I too was an oldish woman, somebody's ex-wife and mother and aunt and grandmother, ordinary and dull. I too was close-faced and crabby-looking, with veiny feet and thick-soled sandals and dyed hair and pants of an unfashionable length. I wanted to go and sit beside her. I would have liked to say something, like 'Hey—sister'. But we both stayed where we were, with our heads down over our pencils, mouthing the words, full of sudden gratitude for the things in our lives that we don't need to talk about, except maybe one day to a stranger.

2007

Dawn Service

WE had never been in the city so early. At Flinders Street a crowd rushed to board the St Kilda Road tram. A big guy in gold rings and bracelets dropped into the seat beside me. 'I've been meaning to go to this for years!' he said in a low, thrilled voice. 'And last night I decided I just *would*!' Most people weren't talking. Strangers exchanged meaningful glances, like conspirators.

The tram stopped outside the National Gallery and everyone poured out into the soft darkness. We surged straight across the road and set out, fast and purposeful, in a southerly direction. Some people pushed their kids in prams, others carried them on their shoulders. We strode across lawns, we streamed along pavements. No one was laughing, no one was shouting or cracking jokes. It was before dawn, and we were going to pay our respects to the dead.

We fetched up against the back of a dense and stationary crowd. We stood on tiptoe and strained our eyes. Faint light barely pierced the clouds. The huge building, with its ridged pillars and vast stone staircase and Egyptian-looking top, bulked weirdly sepia. A man's voice, amplified, floated over our massed heads. He was assuring children that something called 'the Anzac spirit' would get them through the difficulties of their lives.

Who *was* this speaker? Why did he sound so deeply wrong? Was it the hollow, hackneyed nature of the sentiment, or the glossy timbre of his voice, so mellow and patronising?

Next, the invisible speaker turned his attention to the thousands of grown-ups standing in the dark. He addressed us as 'ladies and gentlemen'. He intoned the lines we were expecting: 'They shall grow not old as we that are left grow old. / Age shall not weary them, nor the years condemn.' Two cadets who had distinguished themselves in their studies read worthy thoughts aloud to us in stilted tones, self-conscious, terribly sincere. Their youthful voices came and went on the still-dark air.

The crowd stood in stoic silence. The generators of the fast-food vans, over there in the park beyond the crowd's edges, hummed steadily. We could smell the heating fat.

A bugler played 'The Last Post'. A Welsh choir sang with a brass band. Their voices swelled grandly. After each verse of the song an officer's tiny voice, far away, yelled an order. Gunfire roared. Two little girls in front of me turned to each other in awe. Still we stood with closed mouths. The silence of the crowd was as thick as felt. We stood patiently, respectfully, hopefully. We were waiting for something, the mysterious, nameless thing we had come for.

But the MC's voice, with its fruity intonation, betrayed the pure, pained cry of the bugle. He spoke to us as if we were no more than his audience. The third time he addressed us as 'ladies and gentlemen' a peculiar rage rose up in me. We weren't here to be entertained, to be passive consumers of a professionally produced show. We were not just spectators. We were here to take part in something. We had come as Australians, as each other's countrymen and -women—as citizens.

Now the man urged us to sing the national anthem. The band struck up. As usual it was pitched either too high or low for a mature woman's voice. We sang, or tried to; and then the thing was over. The day had dawned.

If only we had been able to sing a real song, while the light struggled through the cloud cover and Anzac Day began. 'Advance Australia Fair' would not do, in its awkward key, with its clumsy poeticisms and embarrassing claims.

We needed to sing songs we had known since we were children, songs we shouted in our playgrounds or at assembly, standing in lines on the asphalt with our hands on our hearts. What happened to all our hymns? How did we lose 'Jerusalem'? 'I Vow to Thee My Country'? 'O Valiant Hearts'?

Why couldn't we raise our voices and sing out together in solemnity, thousands of us, men and woman and children, unabashed? It was too late in history. Nobody knows the parts. The words have been forgotten. We turned and set out homewards along St Kilda Road, under a grey sky, with our emotions still aching in our throats.

2006

A Party

IN 1966, when I had just started my first high-school teaching job, I ran into some domestic problems and had to find a place to live, in a hurry. I heard someone was vacating a room in a high terrace at the north end of Swanston Street, opposite Melbourne University.

I climbed the stairs to inspect the room. The floor was covered in worn seagrass matting. The fireplace was beyond use. Half the floor space was taken up by a clumsy sink and kitchen bench. It was ugly and mean. But as I stood at the open door, there stirred in me a faint, complex and not entirely disagreeable sensation: I had been here before. Ridiculous.

I had nowhere to sleep. I said, 'I'll take it.'

I moved in my stuff, such as it was, and got on with messing up my life. The not-quite-strangeness of the room might have haunted me, except that the kids in my classes had my number and knew how to make me cry. Each evening I would stagger home, lie on the bed for half an hour, then walk round the corner to Jimmy Watson's and start drinking.

One Saturday a friend from my university college tracked me down. She strode in, looked around the room and started to laugh. 'How the hell did you end up here? This is where we came to that party!'

'What party?'

'You know! In second year! The one where you sat on the floor all night with—'

'Shut up!'

The first night I ever got really, really drunk. I don't remember how I got to the house, or who with. Unflattering light beamed from one bare bulb. There was no music because in those days at parties in someone's room there wasn't music, there was just yelling, and flagons of violent claret. I was a private-school head prefect from Geelong in a twin-set and pleated skirt, and I had never drunk wine in my life; but I wanted to be like the people I was with, whoever the hell they were, so I swigged claret. Sitting cross-legged on the floor, I took my turn at the glass flagon as it passed. Between slugs I sat in a daze of pleasure and gazed up at the underside of the mantelpiece. The room was packed with impressive strangers my age, laughing and bellowing and arguing. They looked like the sort of people I wanted to know, and I seemed at last to have found them.

A student wearing a battered brown leather coat came and sat down on the floor in front of me. He couldn't have known my name, but I knew his without having to ask, because he was *really famous*. We didn't say 'on campus' back then, only Americans used the word 'campus'. We said 'at uni'. His name was John Wishart and he was *really famous at uni*, I had no idea what for, because I only knew people like me who were doing Arts. He was tall and dark and extremely good-looking, with narrow eyes and high cheekbones, below one of which was a perfect, tiny black mole. I don't remember if either of us said anything. But we started to kiss, and we sat there on the matting, leaning towards each other and resting our palms on the floor, and kissed and kissed for hours and hours and hours.

I think.

I don't know where he went, or how I got back to college. The next thing I was leaning over the toilet vomiting, and at the same time I was singing a Joan Baez song, very loudly, and shouting, 'I'M SOOOO HAPPY!' The studious girl who lived down the hall came along softly in her dressing-gown and slippers to see if I was all right. I suppose she must have held my head out of the toilet and wiped up the mess. I couldn't remember anything about the party but it was the best one in the world and I wanted everyone to know that *I had been at it*.

By lunchtime the next day I had stopped being sick but I understood the squalor of life. The sunlight kept hitting me with a hammer. I put on sunglasses and limped across Trinity and past the swimming pool to the caf. I sat down carefully at a table with some friends who were not party girls. They looked at me with distaste, and were about to start reproaching me when one of them broke off and whispered reverently, 'Look. There goes John Wishart.'

I composed my features, and swung round to look. Would he say hello? Shuffling past the end of our table, his bespectacled gaze fixed on his feet, was a short, puny, wretched swot in sagging cords and a jumper with matching beanie obviously knitted by his mother.

My blush faded. 'I thought you said John Wishart.'

'I did! There he goes!'

'Pfff. That's not John Wishart.'

'It is! Everyone knows who John Wishart is! He's the president of the Rationalists' Society!'

My gorge rose. Could *he* have been the man I had kissed? But what about the old leather coat? The dark hair and narrow eyes?

The perfect mole? Was this the derangement of the senses they talked about in French poetry tutes? Had the wonderful party even existed? It was my first existential crisis.

When I recovered I made discreet inquiries. Yes; there were two John Wisharts, one plain and clever, the other beautiful and probably rather dumb. Neither of them ever crossed my path again. But every Wednesday morning, when I drive my granddaughter along Swanston Street to her crèche, she points to the big house opposite Newman College and says, in her ritualistic voice, 'Nanna, that's where you went to a party and had too much to drink, when you were young, in the olden days.'

2004

The Insults of Age

THE insults of age had been piling up for so long that I was almost numb to them. The husband (when I still had one): 'You're not going *out* in that sleeveless top?' The grandchild: 'Nanna, why are your teeth grey?' The pretty young publisher tottering along in her stilettos: 'Are you right on these stairs, Helen?' The flight attendant at the boarding gate: 'And when you do reach your seat, madam, remember to *stow* that little backpack *riiiight* under the seat in front of you!' The grinning red-faced bloke who mutters to the young man taking the seat beside me: 'Bad luck, mate.' The armed child behind the police-station counter unable to conceal her boredom as I describe the man in a balaclava, brandishing a baton, who leapt roaring out of the dark near the station underpass and chased me and my friend all the way home: 'And what were you scared of? Did you think he might hit you with his umbrella?'

Really, it is astonishing how much shit a woman will cop in the interests of civic and domestic order.

But last spring I got a fright. I was speaking about my new book to a university lecture theatre full of journalism students. I had their attention. Everything was rolling along nicely. Somebody asked me a question and I looked down to collect my thoughts. Cut to the young lecturer's face surprisingly close to mine. 'Helen,' he murmured, 'we're going to take you to the medical clinic.' What? *Me?* Apparently, in those few absent moments, of which I still have no memory, I had become confused and distressed; I didn't know where I was or why I was there. He thought I might be having a stroke.

The rest of that afternoon I lay at my ease in an Emergency cubicle at the Royal Melbourne, feeling strangely lighthearted. I kept thinking in wonder, *I've dropped my bundle.* All scans and tests came up clear. Somebody asked me if I'd ever heard of *transient global amnesia*. I was home in time for dinner.

Next morning I took the hospital report to my GP. 'I've been worried about you,' she said. 'It's stress. You are *severely depleted*. Cancel the rest of your publicity tour, and don't go on any planes. You need a serious rest.' I must have looked sceptical. She leaned across the desk, narrowed her eyes, and laid it on the line: 'Helen. *You. Are. Seventy-one.*'

I went home and sulked on the couch for a week, surveying my lengthening past and shortening future.

I had known for years, of course, that beyond a certain age women become invisible in public spaces. The famous erotic gaze is withdrawn. You are no longer, in the eyes of the world, a sexual being. In my experience, though, this forlornness is a passing phase. The sadness of the loss fades and fades. You pass through loneliness and out into a balmy freedom from the heavy labour of self-presentation. Oh, the relief! You have nothing to prove. You can saunter about the world in overalls. Because a lifetime as a woman has taught you to listen, you know how to strike up long, meaty conversations with strangers on trams and trains.

But there is a down side, which, from my convalescent sofa, I dwelt upon with growing irritation. Hard chargers in a hurry begin to patronise you. Your face is lined and your hair is grey, so they think you are weak, deaf, helpless, ignorant and stupid. When they address you they tilt their heads and bare their teeth and adopt a tuneful intonation. It is assumed that you have no opinions and no standards of behaviour, that nothing that happens in your vicinity is any of your business. By the time I had got bored with resting and returned to ordinary life, I found that the shield of feminine passivity I had been holding up against this routine peppering of affronts had splintered into shards.

One warm December evening, a friend and I were strolling along Swanston Street on our way out to dinner. The pavement was packed and our progress was slow. Ahead of us in the crowd we observed with nostalgic pleasure a trio of teenagers striding along, lanky white Australian schoolgirls in gingham dresses and blazers, their ponytails tied high with white ribbons.

One of the girls kept dropping behind her companions to dash about in the moving crowd, causing mysterious jolts and flurries. Parallel with my friend and me, an Asian woman of our age was walking by herself, composed and thoughtful. The revved-up school-girl came romping back against the flow of pedestrians and with a manic grimace thrust her face right into the older woman's. The woman reared back. The girl skipped nimbly across the stream of people and bounded towards her next mark, a woman sitting on a bench—also Asian, also alone and minding her own business. The schoolgirl stopped in front of her and did a little dance of derision, flapping both hands in mocking parody of greeting. I saw the Asian woman look up in fear, and something in me went berserk.

In two strides I was behind the schoolgirl. I reached up, seized her ponytail at the roots and gave it a sharp downward yank. Her head snapped back. In a voice I didn't recognise I snarled, 'Give it a rest, darling.' She twisted to look behind her. Her eyes were bulging, her mouth agape. I let go and she bolted away to her friends. The three of them set off at a run. Their white ribbons went bobbing through the crowd all the way along the City Square and up the steps of the Melbourne Town Hall, where a famous private school was holding its speech night. The thing happened so fast that when I fell into step beside my friend she hadn't even noticed I was gone.

Everyone to whom I described the incident became convulsed with laughter, even lawyers, once they'd pointed out that technically I had assaulted the girl. Only my fourteen-year-old granddaughter was disapproving. 'Don't you think you should have spoken to her? Explained why what she was doing was wrong?' As if. My only regret is that I couldn't see the Asian woman's face at the moment the schoolgirl's head jerked back and her insolent grin turned into a rictus. Now *that* I would really, really like to have seen.

By now my blood was up. At Qantas I approached a check-in kiosk and examined the screen. A busybody in uniform barged up to me, one bossy forefinger extended. 'Are you sure you're flying Qantas and not Jetstar?' Once I would have bitten my lip and said politely, 'Thanks. I'm okay, I think.' Now I turned and raked him with a glare. 'Do I *look* like somebody who doesn't know which airline they're flying?'

A young publicist from a literary award phoned me to deliver tidings that her tragic tone indicated I would find devastating: alas, my book had not been short-listed. 'Thanks for letting me know,' I said in the stoical voice writers have ready for these occasions. But to my astonishment she poured out a stream of the soft, tongue-clicking, cooing noises one makes to a howling toddler whose balloon has popped. I was obliged to cut across her: 'And you can *stop making those sounds*.'

After these trivial but bracing exchanges, my pulse rate was normal, my cheeks were not red. I hadn't thought direct action would be so much fun. Habits of a lifetime peeled away. The world bristled with opportunities for a woman in her seventies to take a stand. I shouted on planes. I fought for my place in queues. I talked to myself out loud in public. I walked along the street singing a little song under my breath: 'Back off. How dare you? Make my day.' I wouldn't say I was on a hair-trigger. I was just primed for action.

I invited an old friend to meet me after work at a certain city bar, a place no longer super fashionable but always reliable. We came down the stairs at 4.30 on a Friday afternoon. Her silver hair shone in the dim room, advertising our low status. The large space was empty except for a small bunch of quiet drinkers near the door. Many couches and armchairs stood in appealing configurations. We walked confidently towards one of them. But a smiling young waiter stepped out from behind the bar and put out one arm. 'Over here.' He urged us away from the comfortable centre of the room, with its gentle lamps and cushions, towards the darkest part at the back, where several tiny café tables and hard, upright chairs were jammed side-on against a dusty curtain.

'Why,' I asked, 'are you putting us way back here?'

'It's our policy,' he said, 'when pairs come in. We put them at tables for two.'

Pairs? Bullshit. 'But we don't want to sit at the back,' I said. 'There's hardly anybody here. We'd like to sit on one of those nice couches.'

'I'm sorry, madam,' said the waiter. 'It's *policy*.'

'Come on,' said my pacific friend. 'Let's just sit here.'

I subsided. We chose a slightly less punitive table and laid our satchels on the floor beside us. With tilted head and toothy smile the waiter said, 'How's your day been, ladies?'

'Not bad, thanks,' I said. 'We're looking forward to a drink.'

He leaned his head and shoulders right into our personal space. 'And how was your shopping?'

That was when I lost it.

'Listen,' I said with a slow, savage calm. 'We don't *want* you to ask us these questions. We want you to be *cool*, and *silent*, like a *real* cocktail waiter.'

The insult rolled off my tongue as smooth as poison. The waiter's smile withered. Then he made a surprising move. He put out his hand to me and said, 'My name's Hugh.'

I shook his hand. 'I'm Helen. This is Anne. Now, in the shortest possible time, will you please get two very dry martinis on to this table?'

He shot away to the bar. My friend with the shining silver hair pursed her lips and raised her eyebrows at me. We waited in silence. Soon young Master Hugh skidded back with the drinks and placed them before us deftly, without further attempts at small talk. We thanked him. The gin worked its magic. For an hour my friend and I talked merrily in our ugly, isolated corner. We declined Hugh's subdued offer of another round, and he brought me the bill. He met my eye. Neither of us smiled, let alone apologised, but between us flickered something benign. His apparent lack of resentment moved me to leave him a rather large tip.

On the tram home I thought of the young waiter with a chastened respect. It came to me that to turn the other cheek, as he had done, was not simply to apply an ancient Christian precept but also to engage in a highly sophisticated psychological manoeuvre. When I got home, I picked up Marilynne Robinson's novel *Gilead* where I'd left off and came upon a remark made by Reverend Ames, the stoical Midwestern Calvinist preacher whose character sweetens and strengthens as he approaches death: 'It is worth living long enough,' he writes, in a letter to the son born to him in his old age, 'to outlast whatever sense of grievance you may acquire.'

I take his point. But my warning stands. Let blood technicians look me in the eye and wish me good morning before they sink a needle into my arm. Let no schoolchild in a gallery stroll between me and the painting I'm gazing at as if I were only air. And let no one, ever again, under any circumstances, put to me or any other woman the moronic question, '*And how was your shopping?*'

2015

In the Wings

LEGS. My God, how many pairs of astonishing legs, women's and men's, are gathering here along the barre, in this vast, pale studio walled with mirrors? White tights reveal muscle and sinew in a pinkish glow. Black tights give a dense, matt profile. Some legs are hidden in loose trackpants. Others are bare: hairy or svelte, slender up to *here*, or chunkily supporting globular glutes and sculpted haunches. And the bellies above them are flat, flat, flat.

This is morning class, compulsory at least four times a week for every member of the company, from the corps de ballet and coryphées all the way up through the soloists and senior soloists to the principal artists.

The ballet master enters, a neat, powerful little blond with a jaw, in dark jeans. Quietly he approaches the central barre. The dancers turn to face him. I wait for him to call them to attention; but without preamble he begins to speak, no louder than if he were in conversation with someone standing right next to him. Out of his mouth pours a soft stream of French words in an Australian accent, illustrated once or twice by a couple of clear but casual movements. The dancers are standing still, watching him intently. I'm filled with alarm. The room is the same size as the main stage of the State Theatre! How can the distant ones hear him? How will they know what he wants them to do? Are they too scared to ask him to speak up?

'Thank you!' he says. A man at a Yamaha upright in the corner launches into some Schumann with a slow beat. The dancers draw themselves up, and begin to work.

And they're all doing the same thing! They know the moves by heart. I relax into the peculiar bliss provoked by the sight of bodies moving in unison.

The higher the rank, it seems, the more individual a dancer's demeanour in class. The lowlier dancers work conscientiously as instructed, while soloists and principals (older, more famous looking) will break off from the routine, adapt it as they please, or sit on the floor in a corner and quietly go through a private series of movements.

Two young men appear to be the pranksters of the class. They horse about near the window. Around them there's a fizz of suppressed hilarity. Tsk. If I were the teacher I'd have pulled them into line by now. One of them is even *eating chewy*. Then I notice that the master himself, completely relaxed as he paces among the dancers and watches them with sharp eyes, is also discreetly chewing.

The music stops, and the master sets out a new list of steps. They must have a name for every movement the human body can make. He murmurs the sequence in a little rhythmic tune. To me it sounds like 'Two jetés, two piqués, brush and brush and brush, plié!'

Everywhere I look I see a wonder. That girl there can't possibly *weigh* anything—a breath of wind would bear her away. What flexibility. What control, what self-command! I have a guilty urge to stare, as one does at a deformity. Aren't that boy's thighs too heavy for his height?—but no, up sails his leg, weightless. A minuscule Chinese girl bends her torso back into such a perfect arc that an arrow might fly from her belly.

Through the huge western window of the studio I can see, only metres away, the balcony of an apartment. A man in shirtsleeves comes out and lights a cigarette. He leans his arms on the balustrade and smokes, with the morning sun in his face, calmly watching the dancers.

All this while, the exercises they're doing have been increasing in speed and intensity. They are virtually fanning with their feet: they're whirring. Their skin gleams with sweat.

I can see the effort. How do their knees take it? My own body tenses in sympathy, in incredulous envy of what they can do. I feel the weight, the strain in my hip joints, just sitting here in the chair.

They break for a brief rest. The stars withdraw. Now the humbler ones from the side barres can get out in front of the mirror for a moment and feast their eyes upon themselves.

I know nothing about ballet. The words *Swan Lake*, to me, are ignorant shorthand for fluttering tutus and rippling arms and melodramatic death throes in some damn castle in Europe. I don't even know the plot. So when I wander in to watch Stephen Heathcote and Madeleine Eastoe rehearse a pas de deux, I'm probably expecting a dusty old thing, all sucked-in cheeks and phoney emoting.

Instead of which I find myself in the presence of a couple of cheerful pragmatists. I enter the room just as Heathcote is shoving his forearms like a forklift under Eastoe's armpits and towing her backwards across the floor on the tips of her shoes, at speed. They are both laughing.

Heathcote is forty, old for a dancer. He is world famous and garlanded with honours, but there is nothing outlandish about his body, only a fine uprightness and strength. His demeanour is that of a bloke you might be standing next to in a supermarket queue: he has a friendly, ordinary manner, very short hair and a grin full of big white teeth.

Eastoe, at twenty-six, is approaching what I'm told are a dancer's peak years. She's a small woman, barely 5'2" at a guess, but, like Heathcote, not at all extreme in shape. Her build, light but strong, reminds me subliminally of someone from my distant past. She calls up in me a strange affection, a desire to choose her as my favourite to watch. Over the five days I spend in the studios, I rack my brains for the source of this recognition, and one morning, when I see her yank her leotard down over her bottom like a kid at the pool, I grasp it: she reminds me of myself and my sisters, when we were thin, muscly legged schoolgirls in the 1950s. This isn't vanity. It's just a measure of how unexaggerated her build is, how close to the everyday; yet she has brought this standard-issue healthy Australian body to a pitch of shapeliness and power by years of concentrated labour that the ordinary teenage girl could barely conceive of, let alone aspire to.

The ballet mistress, in tight black with a ponytail and the soft voice that seems to go with the job, is guiding the dancers through the steps, sharpening and correcting and focusing. Heathcote and Eastoe grin as they work. Their manner suggests that on some level they find their efforts comic, even ludicrous. Repeat, repeat, repeat. Is this the right grip? Would it be better if I did it that way? They seem to have even the backs of their necks under conscious control. Then Heathcote steps up behind Eastoe, seizes her waist, and before I can see what he's doing, she's soaring high above his head, giggling as she flies. He places her lightly back on her feet.

Rain patters on the roof. Again and again they tackle the difficult passage. Heathcote watches himself and Eastoe in the mirror with a fierce concentration. There is a great politeness in the room and he seems to be the source of it. Every time they stop dancing to discuss the steps, the pianist seizes his cryptic crossword and bows his head over it.

Eastoe, her wavy hair escaping in tendrils around her forehead, constantly effaces herself before the more experienced Heathcote. In spite of his genial patience, she is always apologising, as if all the mistakes they make were hers: 'Sorry! Sorry! It's my leg, not the step! It should feel beautiful, but there's something wrong with my arms—I feel retarded!'

He lifts her once more and up she flies—but high in the air on his two hands she loses it and starts to laugh helplessly. He lets her drop, vertical, to his chest and squeezes her tight, like a father playing with a child. Everyone in the room is laughing.

'I have to not get *excited*,' says Eastoe, taking the blame. 'I love that jump. I'll let *you* jump me!'

And this time they get it right. He doesn't 'jump' her, he tosses her, as it were round the corner of himself, and catches her deftly in both arms, cradling her in an intricate folded posture, right across the front of his body. The trust! This whole thing is trust in action.

'Right?' says the ballet mistress. 'Thank you!' The piano strikes up.

And suddenly, with the music, the room changes key. What's happening? 'This,' whispers the young publicist beside me, 'is where she suspects he's having an affair.'

Something has happened to Eastoe's brow: it's low and dark, charged with pain. Heathcote, too, loses his genial smile. His face chills and hardens into defensive anger. They are dancing together, but he is withdrawing from her. His hand, which by all instinctive rules of dance and of love should now be curved round her face, is loitering stiffly by her waist. She seizes it, drags it upwards against his resistance, presses his reluctant palm against her cheek.

The emotional freight of that movement is unbearable. A wave of memory hits me. I want to hide my face; but when I glance at the publicist I see that she too, who has seen this ballet several times, has tears in her eyes.

Through the open door comes a faint rhythmic squeaking. I glance up from this scene of primal suffering and see a male dancer out in the hall, prancing up and down on a tiny, round trampoline and vaguely looking on.

Meanwhile a third dancer, a pretty woman with a broad, gentle brow, quietly enters the studio and goes to the barre along the mirrored back wall. She pulls on a long tulle skirt over her pink tights and glossy new pointe shoes, and begins unobtrusively, while Eastoe and Heathcote are still deep in their anguished pas de deux, to do preparatory stretches.

The publicist whispers to me, 'That's Lisa Bolte. She left to have a baby. She's come back to do a guest role in *La Sylphide*.'

Bolte's arms, as she practises on her own, have a dainty lightness. They flow through the air, like thin water-jets snaking outwards from her shoulder joints. Every move she makes radiates sweetness, lifts the heart. Her facial expressions are introverted and eloquent, like those of someone engaged in a pleasant conversation on a hands-free mobile.

Heathcote and Eastoe turn back into ordinary people, pick up their gear and stroll flat-footed out into the hallway. Bolte's partner, Robert Curran, enters: a pale, long-cheeked, hairy-chested sex bomb who in this role will wear a kilt. The two dancers start work. Within minutes they are both panting and sweating. Bolte goes fleeting across the floor on pointe, her ankles whirring like mad under her delicate skirt. As she dashes past me I can hear her harsh, rhythmic breathing.

They pause to rest. I look at her with curiosity: yes, though she is still, by the standards of the world, a beautifully slender and strong young creature, her torso no longer shows the flat belly of girlhood. She has transcended the flowery innocence of the ballerina, and entered a deeper womanhood. This moves me, somehow. I respect her in a more complex way.

I glance down and notice that a very young dancer has spread out a dark red crocheted shawl on the floor beside me, and is lying on it, doing a series of slow but demanding abdominal exercises. There is no fat on her belly at all. *None*. I gaze at this in slightly disapproving awe.

In the wardrobe department, women—and the odd man—work in silence at big tables, subduing stiff swathes of translucent fabric. Deep in the room stand posts to which are hooked frothy clumps of those crazy-looking notions, tutus. Each one bursts upward in widening layers from its lacy little knickers. Their frills remind me of the tender feathers that Snugglepot and Cuddlepie glued to their bottoms when they disguised themselves as birds to escape the horrid Banksia Men.

A member of the corps de ballet is about to be fitted for her costume. Here she comes, a tall, fine-boned, brown-skinned lass with her hair screwed into a knob on top of her head. These necks they have! The essence of ballet resides in the neck. You can't mistake it. The length, the grace, the exaggerated distance between earlobe and shoulder tip—oh, it's gorgeous.

With the unconcern of one who knows her body is perfect, the girl strips off her baggy cotton garments and stands there in what looks like a black bathing suit. The seamstress pins round her waist a calf-length skirt in many layers, tinted the palest, most watery green. It gushes out from under the hard, narrow little bodice which is being fixed so firmly to her torso that I get anxious: 'Can you *breathe* in that?'

The girl grins and shrugs: 'A little.' 'Enough,' says the seamstress. The milliner reaches for a tiny coronet of georgette petals and plops it on top of the dancer's head. She examines herself in the long mirror: 'I feel like a fairy already!'

Half an hour later I walk out of the building into hot sun, in the wake of three dancers. The middle one is the girl from the fitting room. On either side of her strolls a boy from the corps. I follow them, admiring their slender hips and loose, free, maritime gait. They're dressed in the street clothes you'd see on any slummock their age, but they walk like physical aristocrats, striding easily and with a flow. I speed up to pass them. They're talking about food. 'Chips,' says one. 'Crisps,' replies another. 'Camembert.' At the end of three graceful arms burn three cigarettes.

My last moment of glory this week is to watch two versions of another scene from Graeme Murphy's *Swan Lake*: the Prince's pas de deux with a certain Baroness, the older woman who draws him away from Odette, his innocent young wife. The first pair is Heathcote with fellow principal Lynette Wills. Wills appears in the studio in perfect makeup, a stiffened fringe and a bun. She is everyman's fantasy of the ballerina—ethereal, otherworldly, evolved differently from the rest of us. She is tall, and thin, thin, thin, with tiny breasts and endless limbs and elongated fingers, feet that curve outrageously, immense eyes, pale flawless skin, and a large mouth—features so generous that they threaten to overburden her fragile face. At thirty-three Wills is thought of as a mature dancer. She has not performed for six months since hip surgery, but the flexibility of her joints is terrifying. One admiring critic has described her legs as 'weapons of mass destruction'.

Once the piano starts, the fantasy dissolves and the real woman emerges. She and Stephen Heathcote know each other on a deep professional level: they are two masterly artists in full flower. Their dance, a daring and very sexy sort of tango, is full of adult darkness, a flirtation you know can only end by tearing somebody's heart out.

But then the second pair takes a turn: Matthew Lawrence and Lucinda Dunn. It's astonishing to see how differently they dance the exact same steps. Younger, cheekier, juicier, they bring to the scene a less tragic mood. This Prince and this Baroness are still robust enough to survive whatever they will do to each other. They sizzle, while Heathcote and Wills smoulder. Dunn is more rounded than Wills, even bosomy, but Wills's dancing has a devastating, deep, mature sexiness that you would not imagine residing in such an attenuated body.

This is when I realise that these last five days have made me a convert. I rush straight home and book a flight to Brisbane. I have to see this ballet on stage. I can't bear not to.

That night a violent storm batters Melbourne, uprooting huge elms and wrecking buildings. At 3 a.m. the wind wakes me to thoughts of death and destruction. I can't get back to sleep. It's shaping up to be a night of horror. The only thing that calms me is to think of the dancers, to try to find meaning in them and what they do.

I like to remember how eager and fearless the young ones are, while those in their thirties, already past their peak (though not their prime) and having learnt the painful lessons of injury, seem to radiate reason and patience—yet something in them, too, is still burning, a tough spirit under rigorous self-command.

And it heartens me to recall how, at the end of each morning's class, the dancers split into bunches of four or five and rush in diagonal leaping surges across the studio. Group after group they come, without pause or hesitation, driven by the music in an endless stream of energy. They manifest the tremendous onwardrushingness of life, which has only one destination and yet constantly renews itself, full of a joy that transcends words.

2005

With the exception of 'Whisper and Hum', 'Before Whatever Else Happens' and 'Suburbia', the stories in this collection have previously appeared in the following publications:

'Some Furniture', *Kitchen Table Memoirs*, ABC Books/Harper Collins, 2013

'White Paint and Calico', *Monthly*, 2005

'Dear Mrs Dunkley', *Sincerely*, Women of Letters, Penguin, 2011

'Eight Views of Tim Winton', *Tim Winton: A Celebration*, National Library of Australia, 1999

'Notes from a Brief Friendship', *Singing for All He's Worth: Essays in Honour of Jacob Rosenberg*, Picador, 2011

'From Frogmore, Victoria', *Monthly*, 2007

'My Dear Lift-Rat', *Age*, 2005

'While Not Writing a Book', *Monthly*, 2011

'Red Dog: A Mutiny', *Monthly*, 2012

'Funk Paradise', *Age*, 2011

'Dreams of Her Real Self', *My Mother, My Father*, Allen and Unwin, 2013

'Punishing Karen', *Monthly*, 2005

'The Singular Rosie', *Monthly*, 2014

'The City at Night', *Monthly*, 2012

'The Man in the Dock', *Monthly*, 2012

'On Darkness', (address to Sydney Writers' Festival), *Monthly*, 2015

'The Journey of the Stamp Animals', *Lost Classics,* Vintage Canada, 2002

'Worse Things than Writers Can Invent', *Independent Monthly*, 1995

'How to Marry Your Daughters', *Age*, 2013

'X-ray of a Pianist at Work', *Independent Monthly*, 1994

'Gall and Barefaced Daring', Introduction to *Bush Studies*, Text Publishing, 2012

'The Rules of Engagement', *Monthly*, 2006

'The Rapture of Firsthand Encounters', Introduction to *Forty-One False Starts*, Text Publishing, 2013

'Hit Me', *Monthly*, 2005

'My First Baby', *Elle*, 2000

'Big Brass Bed', *Big Issue*, 2007

'Dawn Service', *Sydney Morning Herald*, 2006

'A Party', *Age*, 2004

'The Insults of Age', *Monthly*, 2015

'In the Wings', *Age*, 2005